HELPING OURSELVES TO POWER

A Handbook for Women on the Skills of Public Life

CU00691148

HELPING OURSELVES TO POWER

*A Handbook for Women
on the Skills of Public Life*

by

SUE SLIPMAN

PERGAMON PRESS

OXFORD · NEW YORK · BEIJING · FRANKFURT
SÃO PAULO · SYDNEY · TOYKO · TORONTO

U.K.	Pergamon Press, Headington Hill Hall, Oxford OX3 0BW, England
U.S.A.	Pergamon Press, Maxwell House, Fairview Park. Elmsford, New York 10523, U.S.A.
PEOPLE'S REPUBLIC OF CHINA	Pergamon Press, Qianmen Hotel, Beijing, People's Republic of China
FEDERAL REPUBLIC OF GERMANY	Pergamon Press, Hammerweg 6, D-6242 Kronberg, Federal Republic of Germany
BRAZIL	Pergamon Editora, Rua Eça de Queiros, 346, CEP 04011, São Paulo, Brazil
AUSTRALIA	Pergamon Press Australia, P.O. Box 544, Potts Point, N.S.W. 2011, Australia
JAPAN	Pergamon Press, 8th Floor, Matsuoka Central Building, 1-7-1 Nishishinjuku, Shinjuku-ku, Tokyo 160, Japan
CANADA	Pergamon Press Canada, Suite 104, 150 Consumers Road, Willowdale, Ontario M2J 1P9, Canada

Copyright © 1986 Sue Slipman

First edition 1986

Library of Congress Cataloging-in-Publication Data
Slipman, Sue.
Helping ourselves to power.
1. Women in politics. 2. Women in public life
3. Self-actualization (Psychology) 4. Assertiveness
(Psychology)   I. Title.
HQ1390.S55   1986   305.4   85.31972

British Library Cataloguing in Publication Data
Slipman, Sue
Helping ourselves to power: a handbook
for women on the skills of public life.
1. Women in politics
I. Title
320′.088042   HQ1236

ISBN 0-80-033363-X (Hard cover)
ISBN 0-08-033889-5 (Flexicover)

Printed in Great Britain by A. Wheaton & Co Ltd, Exeter

"Do you think that women should not have any brains?"
"Brains! A woman with brains is a monstrosity."

I never can understand why men are so terrified of women having special talents. They have no consistency in argument. They are as sure as the Rock of Gibraltar that they have all the mental superiority and that women are weak-minded, feeble conies; then why do they get in such a mad-bull panic at any attempt on the part of women to express themselves? Men strut and blow about themselves all the time without shame. In the matter of women's brain power they organise conditions comparable to a foot race in which they have all the training and the proper shoes and the running pants, while women are taken out of the plough, so to speak, with harness and winkers still on them, and are lucky if they are allowed to start at scratch. Then men bellow that they have won the race, that women never could, it would be against NATURE if they did. Surely, it is not brave to so fear fair play. . . .

Miles Franklin, *My Career Goes Bung,* written in 1902 and published in Virago Classics in 1981.

Acknowledgements

No training manual can claim to be an original work. It comes both from personal experience and from the collaboration on training programmes, conferences and schools with other women. This includes the participants whose comments and criticisms help us improve our techniques and skills as trainers in getting the information across, and in helping them to structure their strategies for growth and confidence building.

I have worked with trainers and administrators in trade unions and professional, voluntary and political organisations for a number of years. My political experience comes from a host of women and men with whom I have collaborated and occasionally crossed swords over the years. There are too many of these to mention, but my thanks go to those I have worked with on training: to Maggie Jones with whom I have run many events for NUPE's women members; to Penny Gostyn whose assistance in Women for Social Democracy is invaluable; to Polly Toynbee and Sue Stapely for providing practical help and fighting power for women.

Pauline Farrar has contributed material to the book in the Meetings Skills sections, but she could not remember whether it was her own work or inadvertently lifted from another trainer's ideas. She, in any case, believes as most of us do that training ideas are meant to be shared and used.

Both Gilly Forryan and the members of the 300 Group Training Committee have greatly helped me as their Chair to sort out a programme of training for boosting women into power and would all want to pay tribute to Lesley Abdela for starting it all.

My colleague Pauline Stephens deserves gratitude not only for typing the manuscript, but for reading it as a woman who wanted to know about its contents. She also laughed at my jokes which was enormously comforting. Martin Stott ran a very observant eye over the work and suggested useful changes. Alice Salkeld and Tiffany Dow helped with some of the research.

Finally, thanks to all the women who give freely of their time and skills to enable other women to become more powerful. For their solidarity is of practical assistance without undue ideological demands: it is available to all women and it aims to change the balance of power in our lives.

Contents

1

Introduction:
Women Need Power

Why Women Need Power

This book is a practical training guide intended to help women, whatever their political views, improve their skills. But the motive for writing it is a political one. I believe that many of our achievements of the last twenty years are under attack, and that we have got to consolidate our gains through achieving positions from which we can more effectively influence policy making.

The title for the introduction was chosen after some hesitation. I know that some women are entirely sceptical about power and reject any notion of women becoming decision makers in what they see as corrupt institutions. But I believe it is crucial that we reach the next stage of our social advance, or risk falling foul of the pressures that threaten us.

The Odds Against Us

Despite success for some women, the majority remain relatively poor, with few job opportunities in low-paid occupations and with little childcare support. More women work and their work is vital to family income, but often they carry the double burden of work and domestic life. After years of hard slog we have changed our aspirations and gained confidence but we have not made a great deal of impact on the way the world is organised.

The world of work is still organised around men's patterns and priorities. Welfare and benefit systems are shaped on the idea that women are dependent upon men and available for unpaid, caring work, in the community. The strain of being a modern woman without the necessary financial and service support is severe.

Further pressure is added by the moralistic reformers who seek to take society back to some mythical 'golden age' of harmony between men and women, when in the separate spheres of power—public for men, domestic for women—contentment was found.

The new moralism eschews permissiveness and promotes the 'normal' family, by which it means a male breadwinner, with dependent wife and two children. It promotes its vision of family life as the bastion of positive social values. In its favour is a human revulsion with the twin excesses of permissiveness, promiscuity and pornography, which are seen to devalue human sexuality and dignity. In reality it would rule through fear, imposing a stern discipline upon social behaviour from the outside to limit individual freedom and choice. In seeking to re-establish authority it requires women to give up their new-found freedom.

It is no accident that the new moralists attack the supply of contraception. In mobilising fears about the effects of chemical contraception upon women's bodies and their future fertility, it undermines women where they are weakest, in their desire to control their own fertility without risking their desire to have children.

I do not feel that the women's movement has coped adequately with these two often conflicting wishes in women. We talk about supporting women's choices, but a lot of our demands upon women assume that they would choose to be childless.

It may well be tempting for women who find their double burden too much of a strain to fall back into a rosy vision of the past. It will take great strength and conviction to resist the pressure.

Yet the new moralists are wrong in their assumptions. The social fabric and the nature of family life has changed. The model of the family they promote is now only 5%* of all households. There are now nearly a million one-parent families, and many newly extended families from second and even third marriages.

Whatever the negative effects of permissiveness, there is also a strong positive side which is vital to women. It gives support to the notion of a pluralist society in which people with different beliefs and politics and lifestyles must all rub along together in a civilised way. It introduced a tolerance for people's choices and sexual identities. Above all it provided recognition that it is not the role of the state to impose a single moral dogma upon its citizens.

Often the freedom was exploited by men at the expense of women. But restricted societies were exploited by men at the expense of women. Only the very few privileged women had the protection in Victorian England that the new moralists claim, and then they bought it at a very high price. At least under a permissive regime, if you were expected to say 'yes' you could also take the power to say 'no' and seek the financial indepedence to allow you to mean it.

For a permissive society to work it has to develop new social qualities:

—the maturity to handle the decentralised power it confers upon its citizens.

*General Household Survey 1981.

—the caring and compassion which have traditionally been supplied by women in the private sphere must be incorporated into public policy making.

—a voluntary attachment from individual citizens to the needs of others, creating the social fabric of the community in a responsible way.

In other words we must get through to the next stage of our quiet revolution: men must change to enable women to be free. Women must become more powerful to effect the change in men and to re-shape society to more human needs.

The Mood of Women in the Eighties

I became committed to training work in the skills of decision making for women after attending a conference organised by the Aspern Institute in 1982. It discussed 'whither women' and its participants, made up of equal numbers of enlightened men and women took two votes on issues of vital importance to women.

The evidence was contradictory. It pointed to massive changes in women's aspirations from the boom economies of the sixties, to a turning point in the mid-seventies as these Western economies went into decline when hard-won welfare services were under attack and more liberal ideas disappeared with the boom. The prognosis was gloomy. Despite this, when the participants were asked to indicate their instincts about the future by voting, the results were revealing.

The first vote was on whether or not women in general would chose to take time out of their working lives to be with young children if they lived in a world in which it would make little difference to their careers. All the men voted that they would not and all the women that they would. The second vote was on whether or not women in general would cave in to the pressures on them to retreat back into the family away from the public domain. All the men voted that they would, all the women that they would not.

I believe it showed both women's determination to advance, despite the odds, and men's reluctance to change, despite their new-found enlightened views.

If that determined mood is to win through, the eighties must be years of consolidation and growth, and they must concentrate on making men change. I do not believe men will change until they are forced to share power with women. They will not be forced to do this until women have the direction and the confidence to take power. Only when women become decision makers, can we bring our priorities into the heart of the currently exclusively male power blocks. Busting these blocks open is now a major priority.

The Current Position

So far women who have broken through have done it in ones and twos. They have often been isolated, undermined and trivialised, when they fight for women. The 'Queen Bee' syndrome developed out of this isolation. But there is now a new breed of woman politician: women who speak on the defence and economy and are taken seriously, and who also change the rules for women. Women who support, encourage and promote other women. Women who are out to change men, not become incorporated by them.

Our society is in a state of change. The legal framework operates as if equal opportunities between men and women are a reality. Witness the way in which divorce law reform was shaped on the premise of women's capacity to be financially independent. Because reality is a far cry from these new assumptions for most women it often seems like a male backlash to punish women who make them feel threatened.

There is a contradiction within feminist thinking. We both want to have freedom and protection from it and our critics have been quick to jump on this. Increasingly we must state our long-term goals clearly, and win an approach towards them that is transitional, encouraging women to take advantage of new opportunities whilst we protect those who are in no position yet to do so.

We must not fall into the trap of condemning the high flyers amongst women because there are women living in poverty with no such advantages. The high flyers are both the pioneers and the role models. More importantly they are the policy shapers who can make a difference to all women's lives.

One woman in the public world is isolated in an often hostile terrain: two women are an alliance and three a campaign. Together we are opening up the chink of space to let women through. We now need to open up the training to pass on the skills we have acquired, through an often hard and humiliating experience, to help women achieve their goals whilst avoiding some of the more painful pitfalls. We need to campaign to persuade those who have not yet taken the first step to power to do so. It is crucial to do this now whilst women are at the crossroads of their choice, so that we look more confidently to the future.

There are many who disagree with me, who loathe 'male institutions' and will have no truck with them. They will see this quest for power as nothing more than absorbing the careerism of men, but they fail to recognise that decision making has been usurped by men and used to shape society to meet male priorities. Men have no right to the institutions of power. Demanding power sharing for women is part of opening it up and dispersing it to greater numbers of people as they grow in stature to handle it responsibly. It is therefore a profoundly desirable democratic development. It may be a high-risk strategy, but it is better than no strategy at all.

The ideas of the women's movement have permeated the thinking of many women who start their sentences with 'I am not a feminist but . . .' and go on to make pro-women statements. We must have confidence that women will use power in a better way than sceptics assume. Wanting women to become powerful is an essential part of supporting policy objectives.

Why Train Women?

If women are determined not to give up, how will we get on? What do we need to help us break through to positions of power and influence in public life? We need to know the mechanics of how society works to brave entry. But more than this we need the confidence to stick it out long enough to learn how to operate within this public sphere. There is no way that a book can create confidence, but it may supply some of the motivation to build it.

This book arises from the experience of running training programmes with women in trade unions, and management, political and voluntary organisations. Such training is aimed at helping women acquire the skills they need to be active in public and professional life.

Women have not been trained to play a role within public life. Our education does not open up the necessary skills and the expectations of peer groups, teachers, families and authority figures provide a formidable obstacle to be overcome. A woman has to deal with both her own self image and that reflected back at her by society. Whereas a man has only his self image to overcome. Women's domestic responsibilities mean there is little time to become involved in organisations around work such as trade unions and professional organisations where men have traditionally learnt their skills. Whilst women are the sustaining fabric of voluntary organisations we are seldom its decision makers. Where we do take office in women's organisations we may learn the skills for public life, but our organisations seldom have the power of patronage to nominate us for public office.

There are also straightforward discriminatory barriers to fight. Committees often have a token woman to give the 'women's point of view' and men then feel they have discharged their responsibilities and can continue to appoint old boys from the club. Even when the odd enlightened body seeks more women they do not always know where to find them.

Dealing With Fear

Whilst training is a collectively organised activity, you learn as an individual. A group can give you support and allow you to recognise that your own feelings of inadequacy and failure are shared by others. It can also help you monitor your progress in overcoming your problems. But you experience the fears and doubts alone. I have chosen to be explicit about fear because I have found it to be a constant problem for most women in all the groups I help train.

Setting out on the public terrain is scary. You experience fear because you expose yourself to failure. But each time you manage to survive you become stronger and more confident. It is also exciting to meet challenges and to grow. Women learn from each other, and support each other, but you stand alone when it is your turn to make the speech or stand for election. Thankfully, friends will celebrate your success or pick you up off the floor when defeat looms.

I hope you do not find it off-putting that I write about fear. It is something you can live through and overcome, but unless you are exceptional it is something you will inevitably experience. If you expect it you may be pleasantly surprised when it does not hit you, but if it does you can be prepared for it and plan how to deal with it. I hope my decision helps rather than hinders you as I could not find another honest way round the problem.

How to Use the Book

The book is split into chapters which deal either with a specific skill or with the framework within which these skills are deployed. Negotiation is a skill you need in every situation, as are assertiveness, communicating and public speaking. Meetings, conferences and the mechanics of the media are the frameworks within which you deploy your skills.

Assertiveness and negotiation are the basis upon which to build. Once you can operate in meetings, you can move on. You need to tackle public speaking before you can intervene in a conference effectively or acquire the control needed for public appearance. Thus the chapters are laid out to take you through a step-by-step training programme. It starts by discussing the nature and organisation of public life and analyses where women have got within it. The conclusion offers some ideas on how, having developed our skills, we can campaign for change.

The training exercises at the end of each chapter are designed for groups rather than individuals, but individuals can use them as mental problems to be worked through. Some exercises are meant to be implemented in real life rather than in simulated conditions, and individuals can certainly tackle these.

If you can find one or set one up, a self-help group will be invaluable. It is more fun to learn in a group. You can share already acquired skills between you, analyse your skill needs and collectively set the goals and targets you want to achieve.

A number of the skills covered in this book are ones with which you will already be familiar. Most women now develop such skills through their own profession, career or life experience. Some do not realise that these skills are transferable, perhaps because the jargon or procedures of public life confuse, mystify and exclude them. Hence, simply learning the procedures and language should unleash your professional confidence in a new direction.

Clearly, few people start from scratch, but most women have to learn to see themselves as skilled people and sadly, many have to learn it over again in every new arena. So, try never to underestimate yourself and your already acquired skills, the more positive you are, the easier it will be to build upon your skills.

You may feel that this book overly reflects my own politics. I have tried not to do this, but inevitably my own experiences come through even at the level of anecdote. No training or education is value-free, but I do not want to preach to women. There is no ideological test of purity that you have to take to benefit from it. You will not have your motivation questioned. I do not think it is wrong for women to want careers in public life and politics, and I see nothing wrong in planning this in a more structured way than hitherto. I want women to succeed whatever their politics. I have concentrated on public life in Britain because that is what I am familiar with. The skills, however, are transferable to any country. Women traditionally come into public activity because they care passionately about a single issue or campaign. We can learn much from our concern, but we rarely end up being decision makers as a result of it. This book grew out of a belief that we must organise ourselves to defend our hard-won gains by opening up power to women in a more systematic way. Even if my fears were not justified, we need the talents and the concerns of women to shape the society of the future.

However you read this handbook—whether as a group or on your own—I hope you will benefit from it personally and become motivated to organise for change.

2

Public Life—What It Is and Where to Find It

There are many paths into decision making in our society. You can find them at a local level through a burning personal concern that takes off, and it is possible for this to lead to assuming power at the highest level. But Cinderella stories are mostly to be found in books, and opportunities for higher public office come more often through design than chance. They are accorded to the people who are in the right place at the right time with the right qualifications for the job. Most of the people who hold some form of public office are men, and most of these are in the right place through the work or profession which qualifies them for the job, which they got in the first place because they had the right qualification for the work or profession which brought them to public notice. Confused? It really is very simple. Public life and decision making is a closed shop, although it is not a conspiracy. Once you are in it you can advance. The closer you get to what are considered matters of great importance, the less likely you are to have access, unless you have the qualifications for the job, and so on. The lesson should be simple. If women want to break through the portals of power, they must do so in a planned and organised way.

Not all areas of decision making exist at such giddy heights. Nor do you have to be professionally qualified, gainfully employed, or male to qualify for them. For those closest to home you need a keen interest and enthusiasm, together with the persistence to break through. If, even in these arenas men currently predominate, it is because what happens higher up the scale of decision making has set a pattern which makes it harder for women throughout.

The very term 'public life' conjures up a vision of the 'great and the good' influencing our decision makers, or loftily setting the ethical basis for life as we know it. The image has little to do with the lives of ordinary women, most of whom do not aspire to such grand heights. Most of the human activity involved in 'public life' happens closer to home. It starts at the boundaries of home life and concerns the workings of the local community and the organisations, both voluntary and statutory, which seek to influence its development.

At every level of our lives decisions are taken that affect us. The Board of Governors at our children's schools decide their opportunities. The District Health Authority and Family Practitioner Committee take decisions which directly affect our health care provision. Our local District and County Councils take decisions about a range of community services from collecting our rubbish through to caring for our elderly relatives. Consumer Councils regulate the services offered to consumers from the Gas supply industry through to Post Office services. Magistrates, should we ever be unlucky enough to meet them in court, make major decisions affecting our lives.

Through voluntary activity in the local community people can become prison visitors and members of the Boards of Housing Associations and other voluntary and community groups. Volunteers can also become counsellors for information and advice agencies from the Marriage Guidance Bureaux to the Citizens' Advice Bureaux, which exist to help citizens cope with the increasingly complex demands of our society.

The range of public appointments and voluntary jobs is vast. Routes into them can be equally diverse. Often local libraries and Citizens' Advice Bureaux will be able to tell you what organisations to contact for details of how to get involved in a particular area of work.

Most women take their first steps into public life through a particular interest or concern. It may be that they attend a meeting at their children's school and find themselves elected as a Parent Governor to its Board of Governors or that by fighting housing problems they get involved in a Tenants' Association. Listening to women's anecdotes it seems chance more often than design that got them going in the first place. Once they have a foot through the door, new opportunities tend to arise. But this hit and miss process has not produced a great influx of women into public life, so the approach has to become more directional.

Many women feel intimidated by the formal procedures which surround public life. They have little experience of meetings or speaking in public and would feel terrified of taking on responsibilities in such a strange arena. They may not know the interconnections between the levels of an organisation, or have a clear view of the structure through which decision making takes place. They may not know what issues are dealt with by what bodies. They may not know that an organisation has different routes to power at different levels within its structure. All these things need to be learnt. The information is available but may need some tracking down.

It would take a vast amount of time to give detailed information on all areas of public life. Here I include the example of the National Health Service, detailing its structure and decision making bodies and giving information on how to get nominated to them. All other organisations can be analysed in a similar way.

REGIONAL HEALTH AUTHORITIES

RHAs are responsible for Regional planning and priorities. They have to balance the needs of different areas, allocate resources to them and monitor performance.

Each RHA has a Chair appointed by the Secretary of State. The Secretary of State appoints a Chair, and 'such number of other members appointed by him as he thinks fit'. The Secretary of State is required to consult the following bodies when making appointments:
—The appropriate District, Metropolitan or County Council.
—The University with which the provision of health services is associated.
—Representative bodies concerned with medicine, or allied professions considered appropriate by the Secretary of State.
—Trade Unions and Voluntary Organisations.
—The Regional Health Authority itself.
The normal number of RHA members is 16 plus a Chair. Of these:
　　4 will be appointed from nominees of local authorities,
　　1 will be a consultant,
　　1 will be a GP,
　　1 will be a nurse, midwife or health visitor,
　　1 will be appointed from nominees of the relevant university,
　　8 will be generalists.

DISTRICT HEALTH AUTHORITIES

DHAs are responsible for administering health care services in their Districts, including the integrated planning, provision and development of primary care and community health services, general hospital services, maternity and child care services, and services for the mentally ill and the mentally handicapped.

The DHA Chair is appointed by the Secretary of State. It normally has 16 members appointed by the Regional Health Authority responsible for it. These include:
　　1 hospital consultant,
　　1 GP,
　　1 nurse, midwife or health visitor,
　　1 university or medical school nominee,
　　4 Local Authority representatives,
　　8 generalists.
Generalists include the Trade Union and Community nominees.

FAMILY PRACTITIONER COMMITTEES

FPCs are responsible for administering the work of local doctors, dentists and opticians working in general practice outside hospitals. These professionals are not direct employees of the National Health Service, but organise themselves into practices and then negotiate contracts with the Health Service. The role of the FPCs is to administer the NHSs part of the contract. They are thus responsible for paying doctors, etc., for reimbursing their staff and surgery costs, for ensuring their premises and qualifications are suitable, for hearing complaints and for regulating the number of practices in an area.

The FPC Chair is appointed by the Secretary of State to whom the FPC is directly responsible. There are 30 other members, half of whom are professionals (8 nominated by the Local Medical Committee, 3 by the Local Dental Committee, 2 by the Local Pharmaceutical Committee, 2 by the Local Optical Committee of which one must be an Ophthalmic Optician and one a Dispensing Optician). The other half of the FPC is nominated by non-professional bodies; 4 by local authorities, 4 by the local DHAs and the remaining 7 after consultation with appropriate bodies such as trade unions and community groups. In addition, one member of the committee must be a qualified nurse, midwife or health visitor.

COMMUNITY HEALTH COUNCILS

CHCs were set up to represent the interests of the public to the decision makers in their health districts. Their duties include reviewing the services and making recommendations for improvement. DHAs have to consult CHCs where major variations in services are being proposed. CHCs can pass on general complaints from the public and advise them on how to make official complaints against a General Practitioner or a hospital.

There are normally between 18–24 members on a CHC. Every Local Authority in the Health District appoints one member, making up half the membership of the CHC. At least one third of members come from non-profit making organisations.

No member of a CHC can serve on the DHA or the RHA at the same time.

The meetings of all these bodies are open to the public and should be widely advertised, although this is rarely done in practise. If you wish to attend such meetings, phone up the offices concerned to get a timetable of meetings.

At a national level separate Ministries keep records and lists of suitably qualified people to serve on the host of advisory bodies, most often known as Quangos (Quasi Autonomous Non-Governmental Organisations). Since 1975 the Public Appointment Unit of the Civil Service Department has drawn up a list of men and women willing to serve on such bodies, as well as Royal Commissions and Committees of enquiry. It also makes appointments to the boards of nationalised industries. You can nominate yourself with the appropriate form from the Department (Form PAU3) Public Appointments Unit, Civil Service Management and Personnel office, Great George Street, London SW1P 3AZ. They also have a Directory of Paid Public Appointments made by Ministers which you can obtain. It is impossible to gauge how much use is made of the PAU lists, so applications should also be made direct to the individual Government Department. If you have contact with an organisation which can nominate you—such as the CBI or the TUC— make sure they do.

Group Exercises

Make up a list of the organisations and public bodies which interest you. Give each member of the group a topic to research and report back on. You will need to find out the structure of the organisation and the methods for appointing its members, the powers and responsibilities they have, and how to get nominated for membership.

Your list could include:

—The Nationalised Industries Boards:

North Scotland Hydroelectric Board

Information from the Scottish Office either Dover House, Whitehall, London SW1A 2AU Tel. 01 233 3000

or New St. Andrew's House, Edinburgh EH1. Tel: 031 556 8400

British Railways

National Bus Company

Information from: The Management and Personnel Office, St. George's Street, London SW1P 3AL. Tel: 01 233 5593

—The Education Service:

Boards of Governors of schools and colleges.

Information from the Local Education Authority.

—Consumer Committees:

National Gas Consumer Council

Electricity Consumer Council

Information either through The Management and Personnel Office or direct to The Department of Energy, Consumer Affairs Division, Thames House, South Millbank, SW1P 4QJ.

Post Office User's Council

Transport User's Consultative Committees
Information from The Management and Personnel Office.

—The Legal Services:

Magistrates. Booklet *Justices of the Peace in England and Wales* from Her Majesty's Stationery Office or the Lord Chancellor's Department, House of Lords, SW1A 0PW.

Prison Visitors

The Parole Board

Information from H.M. Prison Service Headquarters, Abell House, John Islip Street, London SW1P 4LH. Tel: 01 211 3000.

As well as information you can ask for the appropriate nomination forms. If the path through to getting the information is a little confusing, persevere. It is all public information and it is your right to receive it.

3

Women in Public Life:
Where Are We?

A recent report by the Equal Opportunities Commission concludes:

'. . . that the low proportion of women in the public appointments field
as a whole results, not in the main from the imposition of unjustifiable
criteria, but from the use of particular channels through which names
are sought, that is, the heavy reliance on all levels of nominations from
and consultation with outside organisations, and on officials' and
Ministers' personal contact.'*

The evidence bears out both the low numbers of women and the EOC
conclusion.

There are no real surprises in the statistics describing the number of
women in elected office and on public bodies. They are everywhere seriously
under represented. The number of women in Parliament has decreased by
one since 1945 to 25 out of 650 representing 3.5% of the total number of
MPs. In the same period there have been only 24 women Ministers. Things
are slightly better at the European Parliament where with 76 women out of
434 members we register 17.5%. The United Kingdom members of the European Assembly rate only 14.8% women amongst their numbers with 12
women to 69 men. As in most other aspects of women's lives, the UK is trail-
ing behind other European Economic Community member countries.

Even in Local Government, where women have a long history of involvement, the figures are abysmal despite the overall and steady increase they
show. Women now make up 18.4% of councillors in England and Wales. In
1964 the figure was 12%, increasing in 1974 after local government reorgani-
sation to 15.8%. As one might expect the worst under representation comes
in Scotland and Wales and Northern England. In London and the South the
figure is 20–21%.

A recent survey undertaken by West Midlands County Council's Women's

*Women and Public Appointments, Report of an Investigation into Appointments to Public
Bodies, December 1984, EOC.

sub-committee* got a 60% response from Councils. It showed that only 0.4% of women Councillors are leaders of local authorities, i.e. 10 out of 280 local authorities have a woman leader. Only 2.1% of policy and resources committees, 5.7% of finance committees and 5.4% of personnel committees had women chairs. 98 out of 2,711 or 3.6% of women councillors were either leader, deputy leader, secretary or assistant secretary within their party group.

It may be that the arena of political decision making is slower than any other to register the changing circumstances of women's lives. After all most men experience success in a career outside politics before they become involved in local and national government.

Their careers give them a base to develop their expertise; this is often sought by public bodies seeking suitable people to promote to adviser status and so opens up further opportunities for them. Becoming established through a career gives the right kind of credentials with which to seek public office. In addition to expertise, it often leads on to office in the professional organisations covering a particular career. Professional organisations have great power for patronage. They can often directly nominate members to ministers to consider for appointments to public bodies. The other routes men have used to obtain public office is through the trade unions and the TUC which operate in a similar way, nominating their brightest sons of toil for public appointments.

The incidence of public appointments between men and women does bear out this theory in part. The vast majority of those appointed to public office are men. The percentage of women ranges from 29.9% on bodies connected with the Scottish Office to 3.2% on those associated with the Treasury. Thus the theory is confirmed, by the fact that in professions where women predominate over men, men still vastly outnumber them in public appointments. The starkest case is education. Women make up the majority of the teaching profession, but only 11.4% of appointments to bodies set up by the Department of Education and Science. Now admittedly a number of these bodies will deal with scientific and technical areas where few women are to be found in the corresponding professions, but the general point is valid. It is not just weight of numbers within a profession: it is the level at which they are to be found, and here as generally in life success breeds opportunity which breeds success.

Women in the business community are, as everywhere else, notable by their absence. It is difficult to collect statistics about the stage they have reached. Take ICI as an example. In the UK ICI employs 54,490 of whom 14% of 7,678 are women. Out of their 1,750 senior managers, 18 are women. There are no women on any of the eight Divisional Boards of the company. Whilst the recruitment of women to managerial posts has doubled in the past

---

*'Survey of Women Representatives in Local Government' Reference PER/16.14.8/MM available from County Personnel Officer, West Midlands County Council.

few years, it stands at only 10%, and of these only 40% will stay with the company beyond a period of seven years when more senior promotion becomes possible. This compares with 70% of the male intake staying beyond the same period. Despite this ICI offers only the minimum maternity leave decreed by law.*

Whilst parts of the public sector offer better working conditions for women, it is as bad as the private sector in promoting women to its key decision-making bodies. A few industries such as local government and the universities may offer better maternity leave provisions, but there are few women Chief Executives or Vice-Chancellors. The health service may offer equal pay—albeit meaningless because of the sexual segregation of jobs—but very few of the recently appointed District General Managers are women. Despite having generally better employment practices the public sector is not stuffed full of women on its boards and executive committees. In fact there often seems to be little correlation between the kind of employment practices and the number of women making decisions about them. One can only assume that employment practices are better in the public sector because of the general ethos about these in the public sector and because pressures from trade unions are stronger here and likely to find a more sympathetic response. Nevertheless the conclusion must be that they would be better still if more women were responsible for making decisions about them and for negotiating them on the trade union side.

The only nationalised industries with women on the board are below and they only have one woman apiece:

North Scotland Hydroelectric Board, South Scottish Electricity Board, The Post Office, British Airport Authority, British Railways Board and the National Bus Company.

Most women are to be found on public bodies appointed for local duties. Boards of visitors to prisons and parole boards have 900 women out of 2,600 members. These are appointed by the Home Office after local consultation or enquiry. Industrial Tribunals have 2,000 members, 21% of whom are women. National Insurance Tribunals have 4,000 members and 1,200 women. Both the TUC and CBI nominate for Industrial Tribunals from the recommendation of local union and employer organisations; and trade unions nominate about 50% of National Insurance Tribunals.

The evidence shows that more women are coming through the education route into the professions. Women now make up 51.2% of non-advanced students and 35.7% of advanced students within Further Education.

In the Polytechnic sector women represent 45% of full time student enrolments and 23% on sandwich and released courses. In the University sector in 1982–83 women made up 40.6% of all undergraduates and 31.3% of post-

*From *Working Woman*, October 1984, 'Behind the Image', Patience Wheatcroft, Company Profile.

graduates.* These last figures show a steady increase from those of 1965–6
when women made up 27.6 of undergraduates and 20.6 of postgraduates. It
is still true that the representation of women in arts and languages continues
to grow, but so do the percentage in all subjects. In Engineering and Technology they remain a measly 8.6% having more than doubled since 1975.

There is no correlation between the percentage of women graduates in
specific subjects and their representation in the appropriate professional
bodies associated with that subject. The largest representation of women is
in the Hotel Catering and Institutional Management Association where they
make up 47.1% and the lowest in the Institute of Production Engineers
where they make up 0.5%. Between these extremes there is a depressing tale
to tell. Even the Institute of Health Service Administrators can boast only
18.9% women members when over the entire Health Education field women
make up 44.9% of undergraduates. One is entitled to ask "What are they
doing with their qualifications—eating them?"

If the brothers in the closed shop of the professions are not doing well by
their sisters, then what of the brothers in the unions? One look at the figures
in the table below will show you that the claims of trade unions to represent
women are absurd. Even unions where the largest number of members are
women are entirely dominated by men. Even where women by dint of numbers are entitled to the lion's share of executive positions and full-time
officials jobs that share goes to the men. Even in unions where the executives can nominate members through to the TUC and thence to government
for appointment to public bodies and should be nominating women, the jobs
go to the boys.

The overall picture is depressing for women. The old boys network operates in every job, profession and organisation. Women are excluded from
decision making at every level. There are some women who have made it
into the ranks of the great and the good under their own steam. Some get
there because of expertise through a profession, but many are there to give
the 'women's angle' and you only need one woman to do that if the woman's
angle is the domestic aspect of home and family. Not only do you only
require one woman per committee on this basis, there are many committees
advising Government where such an angle is not relevant, thus patronage
quickly becomes patronising, and women can be excluded from 'non-rele-
vant' subject areas.

There is no overt conspiracy to exclude women from public office by election or appointment. For as long as women go on bearing children and
having major responsibility for them it will be easy for them to be excluded.
We already know that the years women spend out of work when their children are young put their careers so far behind those of men that it is virtually
impossible to catch up. Even where women continue working they remain
responsible for domestic organisation and childcare in a way that takes up

* *DES Statistics of Further Education,* England, November 1981, p. 69.

Representation of Women in Trade Unions

Union	Membership			Executive members		Full-time officials		TUC delegates	
	Total	Women	% Women	Total	Women[6]	Total	Women[6]	Total	Women[6]
APEX[5]	95,049	50,594	53.2	15	3 (8)	47	2 (25)	13	5 (7)
ASTMS[1]	390,000	87,750	22.5	22	2 (5)	95	6 (21)	28	3 (6)
BIFU[1]	154,579	78,765	50.9	32	4 (16)	37	7 (19)	19	4 (10)
CPSA[1]	190,347	137,369	72.2	29	4 (21)	14	3 (10)	30	9 (22)
GMBATU[1]	766,744	258,739	33.7	38	1 (13)	287	12 (97)	86	4 (29)
NALGO[1]	766,390	390,859	51.0	71	20 (36)	191	20 (97)	72	23 (37)
NUPE[1]	680,000	455,600	67.0	26	10 (17)	180	12 (120)	34	10 (23)
NUT[6]	250,499	180,179	71.9	41	8 (29)	27	2 (19)	37	10 (27)
NUTGW[4]	76,509	69,319	90.6	15	8 (14)	38	4 (34)	13	10 (12)
TGWU[2]	1,490,555	228,750	15.5	42	1 (6)	500	9 (765)	92	9 (16)
USDAW[3]	392,307	239,170	61.0	18	1 (11)	122	10 (74)	35	5 (21)

Source:
All figures have been supplied by the individual trade unions.

Notes:
[1] Figures are as at January 1985.
[2] Figures are as at December 1984.
[3] Membership figures are as at December 1984; TUC delegates are for the 1984 conference; Executive members and full-time officials are as at January 1985.
[4] Membership figures are as at June 1984; TUC delegates are for the 1984 conference; Executive members and full-time officials are as at January 1985.
[5] Membership figures are as at September 1984.
[6] Figures are as at January 1984.
Figures in brackets show how many women there would be if they were represented according to their share of the membership.

Women and Men in Britain. A Statistical Profile, Equal Opportunities Commission.

all their time outside paid work, making it impossible to take on responsibilities in professional organisations or trade unions in addition to work. Combining children, home life, unpaid domestic work and paid work outside the home are enough for the average woman to play at being Superwoman—few can become Super-Dooper-Woman and take on further commitments. It is easier for women well-off enough to pay for childcare but if the financial constraints don't get them, the mother's guilt will.

For women exclusion from careers can come before they have children. In upwardly mobile married couples, when the call comes for a man to move his job, both he and his firm seem to expect his wife to move with him, and women do. Women often leave careers in which they are just becoming established or may be already progressing, to move to areas where there are no jobs for them in their profession or at their grade. The same thing may happen to couples who are not married, but it rarely happens the other way round.

The pattern is very different for men. While their wives are busy with childcare and home, they are working hard on their careers. Things can get hard for men out there in the daily grind. However, by the time their wives are ready to return to temporarily abandoned careers which they have to resume at often a more junior level than that at which they left them, men have reached a point where they are already established. They can take a more expansive view and pursue interests elsewhere. They are available to consider whatever interesting roles in public life come their way. They may even have time to help with the children and the housework at weekends. Life is simply not long enough to allow a woman to catch up.

It may be that because of domestic commitments women will forever be under represented in the world's decision making bodies, but it is now clear that at the very least there ought to be a lot more of them than there are at the moment. There are women in the contemporary women's movement who do not accept the importance of increasing women's participation in decision making. Some separatists want to set up different organisations for women: but whilst the organisations dominated by men hold the power, concentrating women's energies elsewhere is a way of perpetuating the arrangement.

Getting more women into positions of power and influence is both an end in itself and a means to an end. It is necessary to right the massive social injustice which our exclusion represents, and which creates a total imbalance in the distribution of power between men and women in our society. The decisions taken by men reflect their interests and shape the world to meet their needs: excluding women from power fashions a world in which we cannot succeed. Including women in decision making is a prerequisite of changing social priorities and values.

4

Assertiveness Skills

Understanding Assertive Behaviour

ASSERTION refers to behaviour that involves:

—standing up for your own rights in such a way that you do not violate those of others.
—expressing your needs, wants, opinions, feelings and beliefs in direct, honest and appropriate ways.

NON-ASSERTION refers to behaviour which involves:

—failing to stand up for your rights or doing so in such a way that others can disregard them.
—expressing your needs, wants, opinions, feelings and beliefs in apologetic, diffident or self-effacing ways.
—failing to express honestly your needs, wants, feelings, opinions and beliefs.

AGGRESSION refers to behaviour that consists of:

—standing up for your own rights but doing so in such a way that you violate the rights of other people.
—ignoring or dismissing the needs, wants, opinions, feelings or beliefs of others.
—expressing your own needs, wants and opinions in inappropriate ways.

The major problem for women entering public life is a general lack of confidence. But this lack is not simply due to inexperience, or lack of practice at the skills required in the public domain. For many, many women it is part and parcel of their lack of self-esteem, and consequent inability to make positive choices about their needs or even to feel they have the right to exercise choice over their own lives.

Women do not see themselves as powerful people. Indeed, there is a popular confusion between being powerful and being dominating and oppressive. Most women deny their own power thinking that admitting it will make them seem less 'nice' to others. Many women do not feel in the least power-ful and often have surrendered power over their lives to other people. They may live in situations which deny them power to make choices either through financial constraints or because they have too many responsibilities for meeting other people's needs.

Girls are brought up to nurture others. They learn the lesson early that to gain acceptance they must conform to someone else's idea of proper con-duct. They become acquiescent to other people's demands. They spend much of their lives absorbing other people's tensions and anxieties and easing other people's passage through the world with little attention to their own fears or needs. As wives and mothers they become the family's tower of strength; selfless, coping and ever-present: both martyrs and paragons to the end.

Young girls quickly learn to get what they want through manipulative devices. They learn to signal dissatisfaction with their lot indirectly, through whining or temper tantrums. Adults are much better at keeping their emotional responses hidden, but the patterns of responses are remarkably similar.

Learning self-approval from other people's reponses is an undermining business. It means that you cannot afford to say 'no' to requests and demands through fear of rejection; you cannot accept either compliments or criticism straightforwardly for fear that you are being either manipulated or put down. Given that others learn precisely the same patterns of behaviour, you may well have justified suspicions, but you can only encourage plain dealing if you practice it yourself.

If you are constantly responding to other people's needs rather than deve-loping an awareness of your own, you suffer resentment, anxiety and finally guilt at having demands of your own. Overcoming the trap in which our life experience has caught us, demands positive thinking and positive action.

Whilst this book is not directly concerned with assertiveness training, many of the exercises should help develop assertive behaviour as under-standing and experience increases.

Assertiveness skills are essential for women to begin to live their own lives at all, but they are also the building blocks upon which to construct other skills needed to operate in the public domain.

At the simplest level they will help you to say 'no' when you do not wish to be lumbered with all the unpleasant jobs that no one else wants. To sur-vive you must learn how to say it without feeling guilty, getting aggressive or fearing rejection.

You cannot really seek positions and influence in the public world without recognising yourself as a person who wants greater power. In most cases this does not mean that you are a megalomaniac. You may wish simply to exer-cise greater power over decision making, and to have greater choice in your own life. There is nothing wrong with wanting power. Recognising this is positively healthy. There are far too many people in the world of politics and power who exercise that power irresponsibly or who use it to gratify an ego damaged and thwarted in personal life. It makes them rather dangerous.

Many people confuse assertive behaviour with aggressive behaviour. This is particularly the case for women in public life. Professional women can be seen as overbearing, strident, ruthless or selfish; these are the images that make up stereotypes. Women in the public glare always look confident, resourceful and terrifying. Human beings often react hostilely to people they perceive as having no human failings or fears, but curiously they seem to need to sustain the image as well. Politicians who show human weaknesses, even minimal indecision, lose public confidence. The need for gods to depose is a product of low self-esteem, it completes a circle, and makes it exceptionally hard to break through into becoming confident enough not to need gods.

Assertive behaviour stems from thinking positively about yourself. It means knowing your strengths and weaknesses and respecting your feelings and needs in relation to those of other people. It means being able to accept compliments and genuine criticism and to reject the false. Essentially it means being your own person, rather than relying for security on other people's approval when this makes you do things you do not want to do.

Whilst assertiveness skills are relevant to the skills of public life, not everyone in public life is assertive. You meet exactly the same patterns of behaviour that you find in private life. Much aggression and manipulation is to be found. So, if you want to become involved and stay human paying attention to assertiveness skills will pay off.

For many women the fear of the public domain and activity in it is so great that they will fail to get to stage one without a better self image and improved self esteem. It is, after all, a great risk to take to change your status, to exercise choice and to become a person with demands to make upon the world. It is all too easy to be publicly humiliated out there, and you only risk defeat if you put your head above the parapet.

There are always people around, often men, but sometimes women, who jealously guard the positions of power they have attained and know all the tricks of the trade in making an inexperienced newcomer feel completely incompetent and stupid. You will meet them particularly when you are out to make change and innocently stumble over one of their obsessions. It happens when you are struggling to find expression for an idea half thought through and badly articulated and instead of finding sympathy get a withering put down from the expert. It takes you straight back to school days and the evil teacher who ruled through ridicule. You may experience humiliation from your own feelings of fear when, for example, you dry up on a speech or misunderstand procedures at a conference and thereby fail to get your motion debated. The hot flush of shame that accompanies public humiliation is difficult to take. So too are some of the 'rejections'. Public life can be very competitive, particularly in the political terrain. Failing to get selected for a seat or to win an election are often painful experiences.

If, having read this you are thinking, 'why bother?' the answer is simple, despite the hurdles and fears to be overcome the rewards of doing so are vast. It increases your confidence and self-esteem to feel competent and accomplished. It enhances your life potential to understand your rights as a person and as a citizen. Making a contribution to public life gives you a sense of purpose and direction. It gives you a greater sense of control to know how decisions are made, by whom and how to influence them. The other reason, of course, is to change it, to make it more human and less antagonistic and to make it reflect the needs and wishes of a still silent majority. In my view there will be no major, long-term gains for women until we become more powerful as decision makers who set the agendas for debate and influence the outcome.

Thus to get there we must develop assertiveness skills, but the problem with essays on assertiveness is that they can create as many neuroses as they challenge. No one is assertive all the time or in every situation. Even the most confident people have areas of their lives they find impossible to handle. So, if you feel you have to assert yourself in every situation, you are probably overstrained. You have to start with achievable goals and targets before you can move on. Trying too much at once could prove to be too painful an exercise. Learning assertive behaviour is a process of growth, it probably never stops or achieves a point where you have arrived fearless and confident to tackle anything life can throw at you.

Assertiveness classes often start by getting students to list the most difficult situations they face and then to rate them in order of difficulty. This can raise problems as diverse as an inability to complain over bad service in a restaurant or to ask a doctor for details of a medical complaint, to an inability to refuse to accept responsibility for other people's emotional crises when you really do not feel up to it, or to refuse unwanted sexual advances.

Students are asked to be as specific as possible about their own list. Their task is to work through the list, starting with the least difficult. They practice techniques for learning to overcome their problems, to help them to state their point of view and demands clearly, firmly and politely without being reduced to incoherent rage or silent acquiescence. They practice their methods through role play exercises and then have to undertake tasks in the world outside. Bit by bit they learn that it is not so difficult to confront situations when you feel in control, and their confidence grows.

This book is not about assertiveness training, but it accepts something of the method and applies it to the world of public life skills. You may find it useful to begin your training with sessions in assertiveness. This will depend on the level of experience and confidence of members of your group. Assertiveness skills can be applied and extended and developed through political skills. The objective is to encourage women to see themselves positively as active agents within public life and to supply the information and practice the skills which will help them to progress.

If you want to attend an assertiveness course contact your local education authority for details of the many courses which are now available.

To think positively means that you must see yourself as a person with rights in the situation you are in at any specific time. The first stage is to turn your negative feelings about your abilities into a positive goal to be practiced and attained. As an initial example take the list below and make it positive.

Example

---

1. I could never ask a question at a meeting.
   *At the next committee meeting I will ask the Chair to explain what is meant by the proposal under Item 3 on the agenda.

Now you tackle the following:

---

1. I could never think of proposing myself to take the minutes of the meeting.
2. I simply do not understand what this constitution means.
3. I could never challenge anyone else's opinions at a meeting, even when I strongly disagree with them.
4. I could never refuse to make the tea at committee meetings even though I think we should take it in turns.
5. I do not know enough about this subject to speak to an item of the agenda.
6. I would feel totally ignorant if I told anyone how confused I felt in the meetings.
7. They all seem to know each other and I feel like a terrible outsider. I don't think I will go again.
8. I will never have enough confidence to become a member of the Executive Committee.
9. I never feel I understand the issues enough to make up my mind on which way to vote.

You can construct your own list for every chapter in this book. Simply list your fears and major worries. This in itself gives you a basis for action. It will tell you where you need more practice and experience. If you are working with other people it will often be the first step towards finding strategies to overcome your problems.

5

Negotiation

Negotiation skills are amongst the most valuable you can learn. You will need them at any time you need to strike a bargain or make an agreement. If, in a meeting, you need to agree a compromise between differing points of view you will need to negotiate between the parties to find an acceptable formula. If you are one of the parties concerned you will want the eventual solution to be closer to your position than that of your opponent.

Negotiation is an everyday skill. Despite that it is seen as particularly intimidating to an outsider. Most people assume that it is the stuff of big business deals or the dynamic clash between trade unions and employers, that it represents the hard edge of the world of commerce and high finance. The reality, of course, is different.

It is the process of barter and exchange. Through it the well-prepared and skilful negotiator can exert an influence on the outcome of events. It is a particularly valuable skill for those who possess no overt power but who need to obtain their aims and objectives through argument and discussion.

With a little experience and confidence women make very good negotiators. Take away its mystique and examine it in the light of day and you will recognise it as the method through which women have traditionally exercised their influence. Any mother of a reluctant five year old knows how to negotiate. Indeed it is much harder to negotiate with children who often abandon logic in favour of tears and decibel levels in public places, rather than adults who, at least theoretically, accept persuasion through argument.

When you negotiate you attempt to weave a web of logical argument around your opponents to secure their agreement to your proposals. Having stated your demands you then seek to achieve a settlement which is roughly acceptable to both sides. Imposing a settlement on the other side may seem powerful at the time, but imposed settlements often break down, or breed longer-term conflict. Within this framework of a mutually acceptable outcome, a negotiator tries to achieve agreement as close to her original terms as possible.

Negotiations often take place between people or groups with unequal amounts of power. Interestingly enough, once involved in the negotiation process power is distributed more equally. Once the more powerful participant has made it clear that she wants a mutually acceptable solution, the less powerful can only gain. Over a period of time negotiations can be used to further equalise power providing both parties recognise each other's legitimate rights. It is for this reason that trade unions put so much store on winning negotiating rights from employers.

What is true of trade unions is true of other organisations and individuals. The first stage of winning your objectives is to be recognised as a negotiating partner by the party you seek to influence.

To be a good negotiator you do not need a loud voice or a heavy, physically intimidating presence. Despite the mythology of the trade union world, brain is more impressive than brawn. An incisive mind and control over your material are much more helpful, as is the ability to think on your feet and an empathy for those you may be representing. You do need to clearly state your position and then defend it. This requires a methodical approach to your argument and a grasp of your back-up facts. You must also be able to probe the case put forward by the other side and reveal its weaknesses. You must have the sensitivity to adjust your position just enough to secure agreement in the light of the discussion. You need to be firm enough not to be bounced into agreement by the other side, and abandon your demands. You will seek to influence the other side, working particularly on expressions of sympathy for your position. At all times you must operate in a way that you could justify should the proceedings become public and you need to win public approval for your case.

Whether you are negotiating as an individual or as part of the team, the same rules apply. Preparation must be thorough. Before you engage the other party you should be clear about your objectives. Ask yourself what it is you want and why. What facts support your case? How will you present your case to achieve your aims, given what you know or can find out about the other party? Make a list of the answers to these questions and then ask exactly the same questions from the viewpoint of the other party. When you have a clear view of both sides' objectives, you must decide how far you are willing to compromise.

Having prepared your ground the presentation should be relatively straightforward. Both sides state their case firmly, without hinting that compromise is possible on any item, attempting to set a position of strength from which later movement will be possible and minimal. After the opening bids, negotiators work to sell their viewpoint to the opposition and through this to reveal the real possibilities for compromise on the other side. During this phase possible compromises can be aired, leading later to firm offers. When the parties leave the negotiating table the terms of agreement must be clarified and all details resolved, securing the public commitment of both sides. In the old trade union adage 'get it in writing'. Unless you do misunderstandings can arise either accidentally or as the result of guile. Often disputes arising from negotiations are caused by conflicting understandings of what had been agreed. So, dot the Is and cross the Ts before you leave, or you may have grounds for regret later.

Not all negotiations happen at one sitting. They may take days, or many months. As a negotiator you should never accept an imposed timetable unless it is unavoidable. You can afford to wait for a better settlement. If you want to settle in a hurry, you are likely to accept less than you could otherwise have achieved. But, as with all things, it depends upon your objectives. If you delay too far, you can alienate the other side to such an extent that they call off the whole deal.

If you are negotiating with a team there are some invaluable lessons to learn which can save you from public embarrassment. Always have a manageable number in your team. Decide who is going to play the leading role and do most of the talking for your side. Assign roles to each member of the team and ensure they will accept the authority of the team leader and look to her before they intervene. The roles assigned may be to handle arguments on specific items, or to back up the team leader on particular facts. Everyone must understand and agree to play their part. Make sure that someone is responsible for taking notes of the decisions so you can check your own record if there are later disagreements.

Having your own record of a meeting can be important. A woman trade union official I once knew had started her working life as a shorthand secretary. She was forever tripping managers up by referring to her own verbatim record of what had been said. Employers soon learnt to watch their step when she was around. Her union seemed to think it was worth the fortune in notebooks.

In your team you should never disagree publicly, because the other side will use this for their own ends. In my experience there is always the wally who is likely to state to the world in general that the other side have made a fair point at a time that devastates the case you have carefully put together. In this situation it is difficult to shut the erring member up and undignified to kick them on the shins. On occasions I have done both these things. It is preferable and the accepted practice to ask for a short adjournment to enable you to put the team back together or to throttle the culprit, whichever gives you more comfort. You should not, of course, reveal the object of the adjournment to the other side.

As a negotiation is a formal process you need to hold it in an atmosphere which helps your case. The right venue can be important. Imagine negotiating a loan from your bank manager with him sitting at his desk looking important and you being a supplicant on an uncomfortable chair with no table for your papers. It gives him a massive advantage and keeps you as the supplicant. As far as possible you should use a territory that suits you.

In any team negotiation the spokespeople should sit opposite each other, stressing the equal power of the two sides. If any attempt is made to intimidate your side into accepting an offer, cancel the negotiation. You can always walk out in preference to accepting pressurised settlements. It is, however, unwise to do this at times when it is precisely what the other side wants.

The tactics open to negotiators are as diverse as the inventiveness of the negotiator. You can fix the agenda to keep the other side guessing as to your real intent: you can concentrate your appeal to the least experienced on the other side in order to break their ranks, you can pretend to misunderstand information in order to elicit correct information, and you can attempt to impose a deadline for a decision on the other side. Discovering new tactics can be fun, and with experience you may find that far from being frightening negotiating can be enjoyable.

Notes on Exercises

Most of the exercises which follow the Individual Assessment are role plays. They have been phased to allow you to progress from your own individual assessment to working in pairs, and then to small and then larger groups. They are designed to be a step-by-step approach to developing skills. Whilst they are grouped around the title of 'Negotiating Skills', they should stimulate a range of basic skills upon which to build throughout the training programme, including logical thinking, expressing ideas, arguing for your views, intervening in discussions, and the ability to organise.

Exercises can be run in any quiet venue where you will not be disturbed. Props are minimal, although it would help to have tables and chairs, and writing materials. In each exercise participants are assigned a role and a task. They must reach a conclusion to the problem they have been set. Role play does not test acting ability and no Academy Awards are given, but it does provide a relatively safe context for learning. It is easier to play an assigned role than to be tested as yourself in real life. It feels far less exposed to solve a problem in a simulated environment than to attempt it in a real situation. It also allows you to examine your skills less defensively than you might otherwise feel able to do.

Role plays should be fun, but they need to be run in a disciplined way if participants are to benefit from them. Each exercise should have a time limit set to it. It should be preceded by an explanation of the task so that everyone understands their role and the problem they have to solve. It should be followed by a de-briefing and a discussion of the results. You may find that it helps to have a facilitator to organise you.

The facilitator plays an important role in all the exercises. She sets up the exercise and issues the participants with their instructions. During the course of the exercise she takes notes on the nature of the discussion, the tactics used, and ability of participants to structure a discussion/meeting. She can keep a note of the patterns of contributions, using a chart designed for the purpose, which shows each person's number of contributions. If she wants to be really cruel she can also time them.

The facilitator can intervene in the exercise if it gets out of hand or the participants get stuck. At the end of the exercise she leads the de-briefing, sharing the notes she has made with the group and opening a discussion based on their comments.

Before the exercise she should compile a checklist of the skills that are being tested, making notes against these.

For example:

---

1. Ability to think on one's feet.
2. Skills in putting forward an argument.
3. Skills in answering the other side's arguments.
4. Ability to bluff/present factual material.
5. Firmness in sticking to positions allocated.
6. Creativeness at finding a compromise.
7. Use of assertiveness skills.
8. How well does the team work together?
9. What are the differences between working as individuals and working as a team?
10. Has the final agreement been made clear?

It might be helpful to have one or more observers so you can work in pairs or small groups and use a similar list.

Being a facilitator is a learning experience in itself, because it forces you to evaluate and analyse. For this reason, but also because it is such a potentially powerful role, members of the group should take it in turn.

Chart for Analysing Number of Contributions to Debate

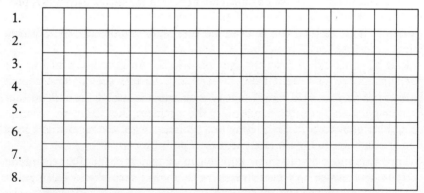

Fill in names at bottom.

Each time someone speaks fill in the appropriate square by their name.

This chart is also useful for showing the reaction of people in different groups. Some people can speak easily in small groups, but experience real problems in large groups. Others feel intimidated by a formally laid out room in which chairs are set out in rows.

You can also use the chart to help you analyse the pattern of contributions of other members on your committee in the Meetings section of the handbook.

Exercises

1. Individual Assessment

(a) Over a period of a week keep a record of all the times you have to reach an agreement on a set of arrangements with another person. Note down the details of the arrangements made and the reasons for reaching agreement. At the end of the week ask yourself the following questions:

—Have I stated my preference on all occasions?

—Have I argued for my preference on all occasions? If not, why not?

—If you have concurred with the other person's preferences has it been (i) on every occasion? (ii) in most cases? (iii) on some occasions?

—Do you feel happy with the compromise(s) made?

If you do this exercise with a group all members should state what their pattern has been. Members of the group should analyse their own and someone else's pattern. The group can then plan what action they can take as individuals to change their pattern if it proves to be unreasonable.

This exercise can be used to chart progress over a period of time.

2. Working in Pairs or Small Groups

(a) Situation: The Head's room in a comprehensive school. Both the head and a parent are present. The meeting is to discuss the conduct of the parent's child who has become, after two calm and productive years in school, a disruptive influence. The child has been truanting, and when at school walking out of classes without permission and being rude to teachers. The head suspects the child may be taking some form of drug. The parent is worried and is aware that the head is, on the whole, kind but will be interested in what the parent is prepared to do to help the child adjust.

The aim of the exercise is to come up with an agreement between parent and head as to how the problem can be resolved.

(b) Situation: You are about to buy a new washing machine and want a reduction in part-exchange for your previous model which is only a few years' old, but now entirely unsuited for your new kitchen. You must discuss with the manager of the showroom the possibilities of such a reduction.

(c) Situation: You are going to the theatre with two friends. Unfortunately, you have not been able to get three tickets together. Only two are together. The third is three rows away. The curtain goes up in 15 minutes. No one wants to sit on their own but you have to resolve the problem so that you can take your seats in the time available.

(d) Situation: A group of parents is working out the timetable for the school run for both mornings and afternoons in the coming week. No one wants to do either Monday morning or Friday afternoons. They also have the following preferences:

   i.   Parent 1: Has a preference for both runs on Tuesday and Wednesday, and is determined not to compromise on Wednesday.

   ii. Parent 2: Can only definitely do Friday morning and Wednesday afternoon, but is prepared to compromise on Monday afternoon, and if pushed to do some of Thursday.

   iii. Parent 3: Can do Monday afternoon and Wednesday morning. Would have difficulty with Thursday, but is prepared to consider it.

First make a chart to help you, and then plan the week. It is best to set a deadline time, say 30 minutes, for finishing the exercise.

(e) Situation: A small community cooperative wants to appoint a full time worker. You are part of the management committee of six. Each member of the management committee has different concepts of the person they require.

   The objectives of each of the six are:

   i.   You want an equal opportunities appointment. Ideally you would like an ethnic minority applicant, given the multi-racial nature of the area.

   ii. You believe very strongly that it would be better to have a woman appointed, given that much of the work is concerned with family support.

   iii. You want a person with professional expertise and management with organising skills.

   iv. You want someone who can do book-keeping and has administrative knowledge.

v. You want someone from the local community whatever their sex or race for practical considerations of availability.

vi. You have no thought out preferences. You are just anxious that the post is filled as soon as possible.

Your task is to draw up a profile of the candidate you would like to see, and a list of the questions you wish to see asked on the application form and at the interview.

3. Exercises for Larger Groups

(a) For 5–16 People.

At a meeting of a Parent–Teacher Association an item of special interest appears on the agenda. A decision is to be made on the colour of curtains to be purchased for the school hall. The facilitator should appoint a chair from the group and give each individual a private instruction, i.e. a colour to argue for, including the chair. Having distributed the colours red, blue, yellow, green, she should start giving more complicated instructions. I include a further 8 instructions. If there are more than 13 simply give the 3 extras the original colours (red, blue, yellow and green).

There is no 'right' answer to this exercise, but the facilitator should note the number of contributions to debate and the content of argument. 30 minutes should be allocated to the exercise.

Extra instructions:

i. You would ideally like blue, but will settle for green.
ii. You would like red, but see yellow as a possible compromise.
iii. You would like orange but bide your time until you can make most impact on the discussion.
iv. You passionately want red to be chosen and are prepared to challenge the chair and take over the meeting to get it.
v. You have an open mind on the colour to be chosen, but believe the debate should be fair and civilised.
vi. You think it is a waste of time to spend money on new curtains but enjoy the conflict in the group and do everything you can to stir it up.
vii. You like blue and green equally, but cannot abide red or yellow.
viii. You have a faint preference for yellow, but your role is to help the chair keep the meeting in order and to take notes.

(b) For 5–16 People

At a meeting of the Parent–Teacher Association a conflict has arisen over an allocation of money raised by the parents group. The parents want the money spent on day trips to sites of historical interest. The teachers group want the money spent on necessities like books. The Head of the school, who is chairing the meeting, does not want to lose the support of the parents but also has sympathy for the teachers' position. They are all aware that the Education Authority intends to cut £20,000 from the school's budget in the next financial year. In the past there has been tacit agreement that all money raised by parents will be used for 'extras'. The Head is aware that if standards are to be maintained, this may have to change.

The facilitator should split the group into parents and teachers. Four people on each side should be given an extra, private instruction.

Parents

i.   You think it is the responsibility of the state to pay for education and have only grudgingly agreed to raise money for extras.

ii. You are worried that if the money is used for books, etc. only the most able children will benefit. As this group is already the school's priority, you are opposed to giving it added advantages. At a pinch you are prepared to see the money used to equip a skills centre.

iii. You are a member of the local history society and have been boasting to your group that the local schools are about to take a much bigger interest in sites of historical importance. You think next year's chairmanship may elude you if your boast is proved idle.

iv. As a parent you are aware that your children are not much interested in historical sites, and have always wanted to upset the parents' plans. You believe the money should be used to fund extras such as trips to the seaside.

Teachers

i.   You have agreed with the teachers' side of the case, but really want the money to fund separate classes for girls in sciences and engineering.

ii. As an activist you are very dubious about money being spent on basic education materials. You have been outvoted by your side but still intend to do anything you can to undermine them in the meeting.

iii. You are passionately committed to changing the policy of the school and ensuring that academic books get adequate funding regardless of the source of money. As Head of the History Department your approach tends to be more academic.

iv. You are a staunch supporter of the Head and share her fears of alienating the parents from working for the good of the school. You do not believe the policy should be changed and have urged the Head to be cautious.

(c) For 7–20 People

A meeting between the trade union and the employer is about to take place. The location is a jam factory which employs 150 people on the production line and 30 managers. 80% of the production line are women, and only 5% managers. The production line works a three shift rota from 7–4, 3–12, 12–8 a.m. and have three weeks' holiday per year. In the past six months the factory has experienced trading difficulties as the demand for jam has slightly fallen. The factory is on an industrial estate on the edge of town.

Before the joint meeting takes place, both sides meet separately in different rooms. The task of the union side is to discuss the list of demands given below that will be put to the employer. They must decide what their priorities are and what arguments they will make in the joint meetings. The TU side elects its steward to chair their side meeting.

The employer's side have received the list of trade union demands. This group must decide what elements they are prepared to concede and which they want to defeat. They must also decide on the arguments they will use. The facilitator appoints the managing director who chairs the employers' meeting.

The facilitator gives each side 30 minutes to discuss their task and then brings them together. The spokespeople then outline to the group as a whole who they intend to argue their case. The facilitator should then invite the group to analyse how effective they would have been in an actual negotiation.

Trade union demands

10% wage increase. Extra week's holiday. Transport into town for those on the evening shift, i.e. 3–12 p.m. The introduction of proper tea breaks. A training programme for women to qualify for management posts. An end to the clocking-on system at the start and end of the shift.

(d) For 8–16 People

In a Local Council the councillors have passed a policy to become 'An Equal Opportunities Employer'. They have instructed the officers of the council to negotiate an agreement with the trade unions on

how such a policy will work. On both the trade union and management sides to the negotiation there are individuals who are opposed
to such agreements. Some of the trade union opponents fear the
effect that keeping records will have on employment patterns and on
civil liberties; some are just plain conservative. The management side
opponents are worried about the impact on their own promotion pro-
spects if women, ethnic minority workers and disabled workers are
encouraged to apply for jobs in higher grades. The managers are
aware that they must act within council policy, but can seek to slow
down negotiations or play on trade union fears so that they can
blame the unions for any breakdown in the negotiation.

On both sides, however, well over half the teams are keen to see an
equal opportunities policy agreed.

The facilitator should ensure that one individual at least on both
sides should be subtly trying to undermine and frustrate the discussions, that a further one is indifferent, that a third is very keen and a
fourth reasonably keen.

The facilitator should allow the separate sides 30 minutes for their
own discussions and a further 30 minutes for joint negotiation.

The elements the teams must consider are:

Wage structures, training opportunities, application forms for
jobs, where adverts are placed, keeping records of all employees,
grievance procedures, sexual harrassment procedures, physical
access to the buildings, maternity leave entitlement.

The groups should seek to end by having a formal written agreement.

6

Meetings Skills

Introduction

The world is run by meetings. Few decisions can be taken or organisations run without them. Given the human ability to waste time or prevaricate, many meetings are long, turgid and extremely boring. The well-known joke of the child whose parents are political activists sums it up. The child is asked "Do you know what a socialist is?" "Yes", says the child, bright as a button, "a socialist is someone who goes to lots of meetings".

Ideally a meeting should be orderly, and conduct its discussions in a manner suited to reaching agreement on the course of action to be taken. In practice few meetings run like this. As a result no one is ever clear what decisions have been taken, and consequently feel little responsibility for carrying them out.

After years of attendance at meetings, you get the very weary feeling that some people have nothing better to do with their time. Meetings make people feel important: "I have a meeting to go to" says the busy person consulting his or her watch. In translation it means, I am a wanted, nay, needed person without whom decisions cannot be made. I am also a person whose time, because it is in demand, is valuable, ergo, I am valuable.

The mystique of public life falls heavily over meetings. In reality, of course, they are only a collection of human beings doing their best to sort out the chaos of information and opinions into plans to be implemented. In theory meetings are a melting pot in which an organisation's members with diverse views have them welded into policies and actions accepted by the organisation as a whole. Often in practice they are the garbage can into which thoughts are thrown never to re-emerge. In some cases they are a sham held to keep the uninitiated happy whilst the officers of an organisation go their own sweet way.

If the objective is to have reasonable meetings which last only as long as they need to and after which everyone is clear about decisions made, planning must go into them.

But before we reach the mechanical details of organising meetings, the first task is to enable women to feel that they have something to contribute

35

to meetings and that they must make the effort to do so. After all there is no point being on a committee unless you intend to make a contribution to it.

First, you must learn your rights and duties. All members of committees have both a right to expect certain things from meetings, but they also have responsibilities towards both the organisation which set up the committee and to other members of the committee.

Their rights should give them adequate notice as to the purpose and content of the meeting. They should expect to get adequate information on which to make informed decisions. They should expect to be able to have their say. Even if their opinions are unpopular they must be given the opportunity to argue for them. Finally, they should expect a record of decisions made at the meeting. Arguing their case may also include putting resolutions and having them voted on by other members of the committee.

Responsibilities towards the organisation include making a commitment to attend scheduled meetings for which adequate notice has been given, unless there are genuine problems, in which case apologies should be sent to the secretary. Committee members should come to meetings prepared by having read the agenda and accompanying documents, and if necessary putting in a prior request for any extra information to be made available at the meeting. Committee members should arrive in good time for the meeting. Being late is annoying for everyone, particularly if the latecomer then demands that an item already discussed be re-raised. If a committee member takes responsibility for anything arising out of a decision at a meeting, she should see that this is fulfilled.

Members of meetings also have responsibilities within the meeting, in the way that they conduct themselves. They should listen to the arguments put by other people in the meeting and carefully consider their own views in light of the discussion. They should take guidance from the chair of the meeting in order that the meeting can be conducted in an orderly fashion. They should not interrupt other speakers, unless it is to seek information. All such requests should be made through the person chairing the meeting.

Knowing your rights in a meeting is important, it allows you to assert yourself without becoming strident and should make it harder for you to be manipulated into making decisions through a process of intimidation. Understanding your responsibilities is just as important for you to be able *to find your own level* within any committee on which you serve.

Learning the skills necessary to work on committees is the most important step you will take in public life. For most people this is precisely what being involved in public life means: contributing through committee work. As a result of this you may need to acquire a range of other skills including public speaking, negotiating and handling the media. The most common single point of entry into public life is through the committee.

For most people committees do not exist in a vacuum. People get involved in organisations because they are committed to the aims and objectives of the organisation. Bit by bit they get drawn into its work and then some bright spark suggests that they should stand for the committee. Then a strange natural law of progression called 'being in the right place at the right time' takes over. You progress from your local group committee, to the regional committee, to a sub-committee of the national structure and finally, to that pinnacle of power—the National Executive Committee. Along the way you may be nominated to represent your organisation on a number of committees of other organisations with which it is connected. Before you know it one committee has begat another in true biblical fashion. I promise you this is the way it works. So if you are going to spend a lot of your life going to meetings and working on committees, it has to be bearable and efficient.

In any training programme dealing with meetings it is important to start with the real experience of the participants. They will all have their own reasons for wanting to attend meetings or to become members of committees and they need to learn the skills that are specific to their needs. Thus the first task of a facilitator is to ask the participants what meetings they attend, what they do at them, and what skills they think they need to help them do it better. You can then progress through the necessary skills at a pace that suits everyone's specific needs.

If you are working on your own without the help of a group ask yourself the same questions, and depending on your answers map out your own learning programme.

Meetings in Context

Not all meetings are the same. The nature of the meeting depends upon the purpose and structure of the organisation which sets it up, and specific task set within this context. The larger and more complicated the organisation, the more it is likely to be formally organised with its own ruling Constitution and sets of rules.

Many organisations have no formal structure. Small organisations, community and women's groups often operate in a very informal way. Some have 'open meetings' allowing any interested person to attend and participate in decision making. Open structures may work well within a particular friendship group, or in the early life of any organisation. Experience shows, however, that informal groupings are open to takeovers by cliques, and are sometimes powerless to protect their less vocal, less bold members. Often instead of being the easy, democratic, all involving groups they claim to be, they can operate in undemocratic ways, excluding far more people than they involve.

Loose structures also have organisational disadvantages. If no one is responsible for particular tasks, records of decisions are often difficult to maintain. Where there are no records, past decisions can be disputed.

Unless an organisation has a firm organisational base it is unlikely either to inspire public confidence and gain support, or to raise funds and achieve its objectives.

None of this means that loose structures are necessarily bad. They often have an immediacy which more formal organisations lack, but few organisations hoping to make an impact in public life can afford to be disorganised. It is simply harder to be well organised in loose groups than in more formal ones.

The structure an organisation adopts becomes its skeleton, it has a major influence on the shape of its body and the flesh of the policies that hang upon it. Thus becoming familiar with the structure of an organisation will tell you a lot about its ethos and purpose. In particular you should seek to know:

—The structure of the organisation through its constitution or rule book, where one exists.
—The specific purpose and task of the committee in question.
—The staffing structure within the organisation servicing the committee.
—The powers of members of the committee.
—The funds available to the committee.

Informal organisations may not have constitutions and written rules, but they will have unwritten patterns of operation, depending upon the characters involved within them. These have to be learnt by a process of osmosis, or 'sitting next to Nelly'—if you can find someone sympathetic enough to explain its methods to you. Whether or not formal rules exist to govern the way decisions are made, the meetings skills described in this chapter will be relevant and necessary. You never know, you may be able to get your group to organise more efficient meetings in time.

The constitution of an organisation outlines its structure. Its rules governing meetings and committees are to be found in its standing orders. The constitution has a legal status and often requires at least two-thirds of the voting membership of the organisation to change it. This is because it enshrines the aims and objectives of an organisation and lays down the ways in which members believe these can best be achieved. When the constitution of an organisation is changed its purpose is either clarified or altered in some way.

The constitution lays down the terms under which decisions can be made. For example, some voluntary organisations have an express section of their constitution which states they cannot take part in political discussion or action. It also lays down who can make the decisions and apportions the power to each of these bodies. For example, a constitution may state that there should be an Executive Committee. It will then state how that Executive Committee is to be either appointed or elected and by whom. It will then outline the powers that committee has, and when it must report back to the body that appointed or elected it and in what form. This may be in the form of a report to an annual general meeting. The constitution will lay down how long the Executive Committee can hold office and what procedures are necessary for its re-appointment or re-election. As a general rule constitutions will cover:

1. The name, aims and objectives of an organisation.
2. Who has the right to join the organisation.
3. The subscription payable to an organisation.
4. The major decision-making bodies of an organisation and their relationships to one another. These may include:

   —The Executive Committee: its powers and remit.
   —Subsequent Regional/Advisory Structures: their powers and remit.
   —The Annual General Meeting or Conference of the Organisation: its powers, timing, location, organisation and timetable.

5. The services the organisation offers its membership.
6. The rights and duties of membership.

The constitution should become your Bible. The person who knows it best can use it best.

To get hold of your copy of the constitution or rules contact the Secretary of the organisation and ask for one. You should automatically get a copy when you join the organisation, but this is often overlooked.

Having got your copy, study it. Examine the section of the constitution which deals with the committee you would like to join. If it is an elected committee, who is it elected by? What do you have to do to get nominated to it? Is there a deadline for nomination to be received? Do you have to submit a statement to accompany your nomination? If so, what kind of statement— biographical or political? Can you fulfil all the requirements needed? If you need a variety of people to nominate you, do you know enough people in the right areas? If not can you get help from other people to meet the requirements?

If the committee is appointed, who appoints it and on what basis can they do so? Is it better to get someone else to write to the appropriate person nominating you for consideration as an appointee or can you nominate yourself? Can you fulfil the requirements that can gain you the appointment?

Learn as much as you can about the committee from the constitution. What powers does it have? What will your rights and responsibilities be? Then make further enquiries. You can always ask the Secretary of the organisation for further details such as where and how often the meetings occur. If the documents are not confidential you can examine minutes of previous meetings and the committee papers attached to them to see the kinds of issues that are dealt with and how decisions are made. You can ask to be put in touch with a member of the committee to have a personal chat with someone who has learnt from experience. If the meetings are not closed you can always attend them as an observer and familiarise yourself with the procedures.

Having got onto your committee what should you expect to happen at a meeting and what form does it take? Firstly you should receive an agenda outlining the business to be discussed and any proposals being made in relation to the business. The agenda also outlines the date, place and time of the meeting. You should also receive the minutes of the previous meeting. The meeting should open with notification of apologies from any members unable to attend. It will then accept the minutes of the previous meeting as a correct record after any amendments have been made. It will then proceed down the agenda items. At the end 'Any Other Business' that needs to be taken will be covered, and the date, place and time of the next meeting agreed.

You should normally expect the meeting to have someone to chair it, someone to take the minutes, and further officials who will report to it. Often these posts make up the officers of an organisation. Sometimes reports are received from paid officials who do not hold executive posts and have no right to vote on decisions.

This is what the agenda will look like:

Agenda for the Meeting of the Somewhere Organisation

The meeting of the Somewhere Organisation will take place on March 23rd 1986 at the Montague Hall, Montague Place at 10.00 a.m.

AGENDA

1. Apologies for Absence.

2. Minutes of the meeting of the Somewhere Organisation held on January 21st 1986.

3. Matters Arising from the Minutes:
   —Appointment of Auditors: To receive a report
   —Annual Training Conference

4. To receive a draft outline of the 1987/8 budget proposals from the Treasurer. Papers to be circulated.

5. To discuss the annual report from the Secretary.

6. To consider the agenda for the Annual General Meeting of the Somewhere Organisation.

7. To consider the proposal that the Somewhere Organisation donates £50.00 to the 'Save the Whale' Campaign, proposed Mr Scales.

8. To consider the proposals that the Somewhere Organisation affiliates to Dirty Deals Incorporated. Proposed Ms B Business.

9. To receive a report from the Social Secretary on the arrangements for the Annual Dinner Dance.

10. Any Other Business.

11. Date of Next Meeting.

When you finally become a member of your committee you should introduce yourself to the chair at the first meeting. The chair will then introduce you to the group. You should be able to get a list of members at the meeting. As soon as you can put names and faces together you should have learnt something about the committee's methods and style of operation. You can either ask the chair to explain anything to you that you do not understand, or find a sympathetic soul to sit next to at your first few meetings who will enlighten you. Once you have acclimatised, you should start to think about the role you want to play on the committee.

When you are clear about what you want to achieve, prepare for it. If you want to submit something to the committee for discussion, is there a deadline for items for the agenda? Do you have to have the agreement of the chair to submit them? Can items be raised at the meeting itself without prior warning? You do not want to be ruled out of order because you get the mechanics wrong.

Be sure you have prepared the ground to receive your proposal. In most cases it is a mistake to raise a proposal unless you know there will be at least some support for it. This means you may have to lobby people about your proposal before you put it on the agenda. You may need the proposal to be seconded to get it discussed at all. Having ensured that there is some support, talk to other members before the meeting to see if you can maximise it. As well as uniting your support, you need to do as much as you can to split your opposition. Do the arithmetic. How many people will definitely vote for you/how many will definitely vote against? How many do you think you can win through argument?

If you cannot win it on the figures you have got, is it possible to put a modified position that can garner more support? You will have to negotiate with other interested people to see if an acceptable compromise is possible.

You are likely to be serving on the committee for a period of time. Once you have acclimatised, there is no need to try to push all your reforms through at once. Indeed too much change at one time makes people feel uneasy. It may be better to plan out a campaign over a period of time and get to first base within your term of office, rather than attempt all and burn out at once. If your proposals cannot gain support can you get support for a working party to consider it in more detail? If so, you at least keep the issues alive and create the space for making an in-depth argument over a period of time. But if you are offered a working party, or referred to another body, are you just being fobbed off? You must be prepared to put some energy into monitoring the progress of the issues you have raised. Try to avoid paranoia whilst having an eye on the bureaucratic inertia that bedevils all organisations at some time. There will be times when you find your ideas welcomed and your proposals accepted with little dissent.

As a member of a committee you must think through your patterns of behaviour in the committee and the image you are creating. Many people operate on a cabbage patch mentality. We all know the person who is the 'youth' voice, or the 'rural' person. Eventually they are only expected to comment on their specialism and are not taken seriously on any other topic. This often happens to people despite themselves and takes time and thought to overcome, but all too often people create it themselves by turning every subject round to their pet hobby horse. As a result of having been President of the National Union of Students I found myself pigeon-holed for many years as the 'youth' voice. The passing years made this a real social embarrassment. Finally it passed, but it taught me that once you have established an image in people's minds it takes a lot to alter it. Thus, be thoughtful about the image you want to create.

There are times when it is impossible to keep out of trouble. If you get involved because you want to change things, you have to put down markers towards change. There may be fights you cannot and should not walk away from. But you do have to try to minimise your chances of ignominious defeat: partly because defeat breeds defeat, unless you are very strong, and partly because being humiliated makes you feel bad and smashes your confidence unless you happen to be a masochist. If you are in this situation, try to ensure that you will at least gain some allies before defeat yawns up to greet you. It will make you feel better while you try to recover your dignity.

A committee can be an enclosed community. You will get to know the other people on it really well in the role they play on it. You will get to be able to judge how they will jump on issues and how to approach them to gain support, and whether or not it is worth your while to do so. Then you will have become an old hand at the committee business.

For the first few meetings just sit back and note the kinds of contributions that people make to see if you can discern a pattern to the contributions they make and how far you agree with them.

Chairing a Meeting

The task of the chair changes emphasis in different kinds of meetings. In a small group of relaxed people it can be a casual undertaking. In a very fraught group where there are strong disagreements it requires far more concentration. In the former case the chair may contribute a lot—in the latter very little, but the task that has to be accomplished remains the same.

Throughout I use the term 'chair' but most formal organisations persist in using the term 'chairman' claiming it to be functional rather than gender descriptive. Thus as a woman you will be called 'madame chairman'. Some organisations use the term 'chairwoman' when a woman takes the chair. I use the term chair because I agree that it should describe a function and delete the 'man' because I do not believe it should be sex specific. Many feminists use the term 'chairperson'.

Chairing a meeting puts a particular responsibility on people. The chair is in a very strong position. She determines who will speak, and often the weight and time given to issues. The attitude of the chair can be very influential on the outcome of decisions.

The role of the chair is to see that the order of business on the agenda is followed and that issues are properly aired, with all points of view having reasonable time for expression. At the same time the chair must ensure that the business is completed in the time allocated. There is thus a discipline on the person chairing a meeting which is lacking on any individual member of the meeting.

The objective of an individual member of the meeting is to express their point of view and to attempt to win support for their position in particular debates. The objective of a chair, no matter how partisan their own views might be, is to ensure adequate debate and a reasonable concensus of opinion wherever possible.

Most meetings are very badly chaired. They are allowed to ramble around the topics on the agenda. Some chairs allow people to re-raise items at will that have in theory already been decided. They often lack even the semblance of control over a meeting. As a result all members of the meeting emerge later, blinking into the light feeling disgruntled and irritated. As a result of bad chairing, chaos can reign in meetings, and in time, attendance will fall off. Even where members take advantage of the same bad chairing, they always in the end resent it when others learn the same tricks. There is a real feeling of dissipation and complete lack of motivation after a sloppily chaired meeting.

If the sloth makes a bad chair, the disciplinarian can be worse. Sticking to the agenda and keeping an eye on the clock are necessary parts of chairing skills, but so is recognising the purpose of a meeting and the responsibility towards the members of that meeting. People will be equally disgruntled if they feel rail-roaded into making decisions without enough discussion and thought. Such a rigid style will also totally intimidate the less vocal, less experienced members of the meeting. In which case they are effectively barred from speaking their mind and true concensus can never be claimed to have been achieved.

The chair then, has to combine the skills of controlling the agenda with an empathy for the issues to be discussed and the people discussing them. The most common mistakes are to be either too hard and rigid or too relaxed and sloppy. But given that we are all human it is easy to err from the ideal. If occasionally you do, you will find that people can be very forgiving.

Not even the most experienced chair can handle a meeting that is dedicated to anarchy and chaos. I once chaired a women's group with an open structure and a possible attendance of 62. Two or three disruptive people could wreck an entire meeting and no one seemed prepared to do anything about it.

I ended a year as chair feeling as though I could have taught Ghengis Khan a few tricks on rule through fear. At the time it seemed the only way to get people to make decisions—but it was an unhappy experience for all concerned, and is not to be recommended as a method.

The chair often has an official responsibility for safeguarding the constitution and interpreting its terms. Most small meetings do not operate in a formal enough way to call upon this power often, but there are few conferences without a quota of constitutional experts and procedural bores, who sorely try the life of the person chairing. Even in a small meeting, however, it is a boost to confidence to know what you can and cannot do in any given emergency. It is for this reason that the chair should know her powers under the constitution.

You may have to know how to deal with 'points of order'. These are not as frightening as they sound, they are literally points people wish to make concerning the conduct and procedure of the meeting. I deal with these in detail in the chapter on Conferences, as it is here that you will come across them most. Business within any formal meeting is conducted in the terms of the organisation's Standing Orders and it is the job of the chair to ensure that these are respected to promote an orderly gathering.

To prepare well for a meeting, the chair should think about the agenda beforehand. The chair should have an idea of the items that need little deliberation and those which are controversial.

She should have a notional time limit for each item, which she can and must adjust in the light of people's real concerns as they emerge on the day. The notional timings give a positive framework to the meeting within which greater flexibility can be reached. They also allow the chair to negotiate with the meeting in order to gain its consent to be chaired. If she proposes and gains agreement on a deadline for the meeting to finish, she can always remind members of this when the discussion goes astray and she wishes to bring them back to the topic on the agenda. This acts as a form of discipline upon the meeting and is more effective if there has been prior agreement to the terms.

When you take an agenda and add notional timings to its items, the form of the meeting begins to take shape. It may be that some members have a long way to travel home and buses or trains to catch. They may feel totally disgruntled if the really controversial item for which they made the effort to attend is not to be raised until after their last train has departed. If you do not deliberately want to manipulate the meeting, you need to make sure that the item is taken when all members are present.

Decisions at meetings are taken in a variety of forms. These can include:

—A formal motion with or without amendments.
—A recommendation made within a report.
—A proposal outlined as an item of business on the agenda.

However decisions are framed, committee members have the right to amend them or send them back for further consideration. Some organisations take formal votes on every item; others work by concensus only, so that any dissent ensures a proposal will fail. Most organisations use a mixture of both. Where an organisation is cohesive and working well, there will be few formal votes taken except on the most controversial items. Many decisions are made 'Nem Com' (with no dissent).

Where there are formal motions and amendments, these are often 'moved' and 'seconded'. In other words a proposing speech is made to introduce the motion, followed by a back-up speech from a supporter adding further information. This practise is now slightly antiquated in the context of a small meeting where a proposing speech suffices, but it is still used in formal debates. Amendments to the motion are moved in logical order by their proposers. After a general discussion the chair will take a vote after the proposers have had a chance to sum up their views.

As well as formal responsibilities, the chair has some informal ones. She is the person in control of the meeting, and has a special responsibility for attempting to encourage the quiet members to speak and for introducing new members. She also has to keep the boldest in check. These may be people who contribute a great deal and often, but the chair must keep a balance between voluble, if valuable committee members and the shy and retiring.

The chair also has a responsibility outside the meeting itself. She will often be involved in agreeing the agenda with the secretary, and perhaps in liaising with any full-time staff member to ensure reports are ready on time. She may be liaising with committee members to ensure she understands proposals they wish to make. She may have responsibility for ensuring that decisions made are implemented. The extent of her responsibilities will depend upon the nature and tradition of the organisation. Some chairs really are figureheads operating in an honorary capacity.

Minute Taking

I had contemplated not having a section on minute taking at all as in my experience the only women present at meetings are asked to take the minutes. I refuse on principle, but I did serve my time as minute taker and recognise that it is a useful basic skill which will help you progress. It is important to have clear and precise minutes. Without them you will spend the next meeting arguing about what you really agreed and who was going to do it. Minutes are essential for good and efficient organisation—too few organisations keep them properly.

The state of the minutes often tell you a lot about the state of the organisation.

Learning to take minutes will help you in many other situations. It teaches you to summarise ideas quickly and to analyse debates. You also become far more aware of the balance of opinions and the pattern of views. This in turn helps you organise your own lobbying later on.

Taking minutes can concentrate the mind on the components and mechanics of a meeting and can be a valuable learning exercise in itself. So, if asked to do the minutes you may find it valuable, you may even volunteer, but make sure it is a job with a get-out clause and a time limit, in case it becomes a trap.

Essentially the form of the minutes follows that of the agenda. You should record the name and the date of the committee and where it is being held. The items on the minutes are then as follows:

1. Names of members present, plus any other people present (marked as in attendance).
2. Names of members who have sent apologies.
3. Any comment on the minutes of the previous meeting along with its date.
4. Item by item following the agenda noting any formal motions and amendment put forward for discussion and the decisions taken.
5. Any other relevant business.
6. The time, date and place of the next committee meeting.

It is unusual and unnecessary to record the details of the debate unless a member has specifically asked for their remarks to be recorded and the meeting has agreed that this should be done. You may find it helpful to include an action column down the right-hand side of the page placing alongside any decision the initials of the person who has agreed to deal with it.

Resolutions and Amendments

A resolution is a formal device around which debate is structured. The resolution is a short statement outlining a policy position and can be on any subject relevant to the organisation, which the chair accepts as being in line with the constitution's terms. All resolutions are open to amendment. There may be special rules that govern the date or time by which resolutions have to be received to get to the agenda of a meeting. There may be rules governing who has the right to put them, but as a rule of thumb all voting members of a committee should be able to put resolutions. Resolutions may simply be an expression of opinion, or they may commit the organisation to spending money or to some action.

For example, a women's organisation has the following motions for discussion on its agenda:

(a) The Executive Committee notes the publication of the Government's

Green Paper on Divorce Reform, and expresses its concern on the future position of older women whose expectation of financial support may be cut without any compensating job opportunities.

(b) The Executive Council notes the publication of the Government's Green Paper on Divorce Reform and resolves to join all other organisations in a vigorous campaign against the proposed changes.

(c) The Executive Council notes the publication of the Government's Green Paper on Divorce Reform and resolves to produce a briefing on its contents to send to all affiliated groups.

In this situation motions (b) and (c) are likely to be taken as amendments to motion (a). If the movers of all three motions could agree amongst themselves on a single resolution to put to the meeting they can 'composite' their position, but they may judge that it would be better to put them separately in case there is a body of opposition within the meeting to the ideas in motion (b) which would otherwise have accepted motions (a) and (c).

When you move a motion you must give your reasons for making your proposal as clearly and concisely as possible. People on your committee may never have heard this argument before and will need to be convinced. Thus even if the pros and cons are crystal clear to you, you must assume that they are as clear as mud to everyone else and seek to provide them with enough information to convince them without blinding them with statistics and science.

Avoiding Manipulation

It is fairly easy for a meeting to be manipulated. It can be done either through chaos and lack of organisation, or through too tight a structure. It can be done either by accident or design.

In the first example, you may not get minutes for the previous meeting. They may be laid on the table at the meeting itself, ensuring that no one has had time to read them and check up on details at issue. The minutes may be vague or skate round important issues, obscuring them. The minutes may be inaccurate. The meeting itself may be badly chaired so that everyone speaks at once and no one has a clue what has been decided on any topic. Essential information may have been omitted or produced too late to be of any value. If the elected officers of a committee are weak, the full-time officials who service it may start running the show so that the committee members become puppets for their wishes.

In the second example efficiency takes over from participation. You will get the minutes on time, and they will be so detailed it is difficult to find the time to go through them in detail. On each item on the agenda there will be a mass of information. The agenda may indicate that a particular paper's recommendations are to be accepted and the paper may be so dense that its recommendations are hidden away in tightly written paragraphs. If officials control the volume and content of information they have a great deal of power. The agenda may be so loaded with trivia that should be discussed elsewhere that you are forced to make snap decisions on major items because of the shortness of time. The chair may be so authoritarian that committee members get scared to raise their doubts in case they end up looking silly.

In the first case you must ensure that the meeting is better organised. This may mean totally streamlining and overhauling the organisation as a whole. In the second you must organise outside the meeting for change. Undoubtedly other members of the committee will feel the same as you. They will suspect they are being duped but have been too nervous to question the proceedings. In extreme cases you may need to lobby within the organisation as a whole for change. If the whole organisation is corrupt beyond reform, why not stop banging your head against a brick wall, leave it and indulge in some leisure time. You have no idea how good it will feel.

In most cases manipulative techniques are historical accidents and not the product of design, but as a general rule if you feel paranoid, people may really be out to get you. In either case you will need to organise with others outside the power circle to put matters to rights.

Meeting Skills Exercises

1. Each member of the group should write a list of the kinds of meetings they have attended in their lives. They should then make a list of any features in common between the meetings and then any unusual features of the meetings they have attended. These lists should then be compared.

2. Each member of the group should describe the meetings they attend now and why they go to them. In other words what is it they want to achieve both through the meetings they attend and inside them. What are the things they find difficult to do and why? What are the things that happen in a meeting that leave them bewildered? On the basis of this discussion you can start to plan your training programme.

3. You should discuss what rights you feel members of a meeting have, writing a list on a large sheet of paper. Then match these with a list of responsibilities. Do these lists sound like the practice you are used to in meetings?

4. Treat your skills group as a formal meeting. Construct formal agendas with minutes from the previous meeting, reports from group members, etc. Formulate decisions into resolutions which can be

recorded. Ask people to take various roles such as minute taker and chair and rotate these roles around various members of the group so that everyone eventually gets a turn.

5. Some organisations have committee meetings which are open to the public. This is true of both local government and local district health authorities. As an interested member of the public you can also apply to the Clerk of the Council, or the District Administrator in the case of the DHAs, to receive committee documents. You should at least be able to get hold of agendas and minutes although some committee documents may be counted as 'private and confidential'. You can do a two part exercise by both attending the meeting, and then hold your own meeting, using the same papers having appointed your own chair and minute taker. It is interesting to see how differently your meeting develops from that which happened at the council. You can then analyse why your meeting turned out differently. It is useful to get some group members to act as observers at your version of the meeting so that they can take notes on the points of departure from the real meeting. They should, of course, have been at the real meeting.

6. When you attend meetings of any organisation take a check list of points to look for with you:
   (a) Is there a proper agenda for the meeting? Proper minutes? Has the agenda let you know precisely what will be discussed?
   (b) Is the meeting kept strictly to the agenda?
   (c) How do people get to speak at the meeting?
   (d) Is the discussion adequate/overlong/informative/boring? Would you have changed your mind on the basis of the discussion?
   (e) Does the chair make an effort to bring people into discussion?
   (f) Does everyone appear satisfied with the results of the meeting?
   (g) If there are officers at the meeting how much do they contribute, and at what points?
   (h) Are formal resolutions taken during debate? If so, in what form are these presented?
   (i) What kind of matters are raised as 'Any Other Business'?
   (j) Did you leave the meeting feeling you would be happy to attend again? If not, why not?

7. If you have completed the above survey of the meeting write a short paper, i.e. one side of A4 on how the meeting could be improved. Describe the meeting to the group and present your paper on how it could be improved.

8. When learning to chair a meeting, analyse the specific problems you face. Is there a committee member who disrupts the meeting and

makes your life as chair impossible? If so, how are you going to handle the situation? Would a quiet chat suffice, or do you need to discuss this with other members of the committee to put pressure on to get her to behave better? If so, who are your allies and who should not be approached? In this way when you have defined the problem you can construct a course of action to overcome it. If you are working in a group you can ask another member to play the role of the disrupter to allow you to practise your techniques for dealing with the situation.

9. *Minute Taking*

   (a) To become proficient at minute taking, take unofficial minutes at any meeting you attend and compare them with the official minutes. Note whether or not you think the official minutes are accurate.
   (b) Are they a fair record according to your notes? Do they clarify or obscure what took place at the meeting?
   (c) Try writing down minutes of a meeting some time after it has taken place and then compare them with the official record. How much had you forgotten?

10. *A Meeting Skills Game*

   You are in a meeting of the local community organisation discussing plans for the coming year. Each person is given a card with one term on it to which they must allude during the discussion. These terms can be anything appropriate such as: Mother and Baby Club. Teenagers. The Committee. Recreation. The Churches. Rural Groups. Vandalism. Drug Abuse. The Spring Fete.

   During the allocated meeting time, say 30 minutes, participants work in pairs. One partner is given the skills list below, the other is given the skills check list on which to make comments. The idea is that during the meeting as well as talking about her own 'term' one half of the pair must practise particular meeting skills, whilst the other half assesses how well she does it.

   This exercise will make you far more aware of your own and your partner's level of skill. Each partner receives the following instructions:

   Instructions to Practising Partner

   In the meeting you should seek to practise as many of the following skills as possible, as mastering them contributes towards successful meetings:

   (a) Giving an opinion.
   (b) Disagreeing.

(c) Making a suggestion.
(d) Introducing your own topic or ideas.
(e) Summarising what has been said.
(f) Resisting being interrupted.
(g) Developing a topic or ideas more deeply.
(h) Giving support to others.
(i) Closing a subject down.
(j) Bringing discussion back to the point.
(k) Asking for information.
(l) Bringing in another member.
(m) Seeking clarification.
(n) Drawing attention to what is happening in the group.
(o) Insisting on an answer.
(p) Testing for agreement.
(q) Getting your own view accepted.

Instructions to Observing Partner

Watch your group member closely and record their activity during the discussion. Note their words and their non-verbal behaviour (nodding, body language, finger-wagging, etc.) as they try to practise the skills listed.

	Words	Non-verbal behaviour
Giving an opinion		
Disagreeing		
Making a suggestion		
Introducing your own topic		
Summarising what has been said		
Resisting being interrupted		
Developing a topic more deeply		
Giving support to others		
Closing a subject down		
Bringing discussion back to the point		
Asking for information		
Bringing in another member		
Seeking clarification		
Drawing attention to what is happening in the group		
Insisting on an answer		
Testing for agreement		

7

Public Speaking

Having taken the assault course on meetings, and learnt to negotiate for survival, the time has come to open your mouth a little wider. For most people the prospect of speaking in public is far worse than going to the dentist. It is frightening. It can make you faint with dread; induce knocking of the knees, and symptoms of sickness in the stomach. There are those who take to it naturally, but most have to learn to do it and the learning can be painful.

Why is public speaking so universally feared? Perhaps it is because it exposes you and your ideas to such open scrutiny without providing any cover to hide behind. But no matter how difficult a barrier it is to overcome, public and political life require you to communicate ideas to others, often in quite formal surroundings. Hence public speaking must be learnt. For most people the 'stick and carrot' method works in time. The stick is the need to progress through the hurdles of public life, the carrot is the massive boost to confidence you receive when ideas, well communicated, change people's minds. There is little else so ego boosting as a well-delivered speech during which you feel in contact with and appreciated by an audience.

You will also get used to speaking to larger and larger groups over a period of time. In your committee meetings you will know people, as you may in other small arenas. You will often be sitting around a table or in a circle, in equal position to others. You must learn to make the transition from this to standing in front of a group of people, probably sitting in serried rows facing you, when all eyes will be trained upon you. There is no way this transition can be made easy, but it may become less painful when you realise that everyone who has done it feels they failed badly at first and found it an often humiliating experience. Try asking them. Many experienced and entertaining public speakers will get sick with nerves before a speech. But, if you watch them deliver it they will look cool, controlled and confident. If you watch very carefully you can sometimes see that their hands are shaking, but their voices sound fine and an average observer will detect no hint of a problem. This knowledge should be your saving grace: even if you feel terrible, just because you are up there doing it, you will look confident to most people. This should help you survive until you build your confidence through practise.

My experience is no different to anyone else. The first time I spoke in public was terrifying. It was in a Students' Union meeting where I was proposing myself for election to represent my union at a student conference. I chain smoked and chewed my nails, and blurted out my statement in a mental haze. Afterwards I felt the hot flush of shame at having made a public idiot of myself. I remember wanting someone—anyone—to tell me I had done okay, but was too scared to ask. I got elected to the delegation and it turned out that my friends had assumed I had been doing that sort of thing from the cradle, so did not think that I needed any reassurance. My own feelings about public speaking gradually got better, but it took a long time before I felt relaxed doing it and even longer before I enjoyed it.

If you ask around you will hear many similar stories. So, the thing to do is hold your nose and jump in at the deep end. We can, however, provide water wings for beginners.

The speech you give can only be as good as your preparation for it. As soon as you know you will have to give a talk or presentation, get the date firmly fixed in your mind. As the time approaches think through your subject and make notes on your thoughts. Discuss the issues you will cover with friends or in your group, until you feel confident about your ideas. Try talking to those who will disagree with you to thoroughly test out your ideas, for those who disagree with you are likely to put you under greater scrutiny than those who naturally want you to do well. Discussing with opponents will help you sharpen up your presentation for an audience that owes you no special loyalty.

You must also think about the kind of audience you will be addressing. Are they like-minded people, or have they invited you to prove you wrong? Beginners should perhaps only accept invitations from more sympathetic sources. Coping with one problem at a time is enough. But the nature of your audience will determine the shape and style of your presentation. If, for example, you will be talking to a general-interest rather than specialist group you cannot assume a high level of knowledge about the subject, whereas a specialist group could be far more taxing of your own expertise.

With time and practice the style of your delivery becomes just as important to you as content. After all you are doing it to communicate ideas, not just to survive the experience, or for your own enjoyment. You have to win and persuade an audience of your ideas. The most you can expect from them is that they will give you a chance: they have shown enough interest in what you have to say to turn up to listen to you, the rest is up to you.

We are all aware of examples of bad public speaking. Just think back to all those prize day ceremonies at school and remember the droning on of worthies and the intense irritation and pins and needles they prompted. If you went on to college you will remember the lecturer who could not lecture, and if you did not the politician who preached or the clergyman who did not. Clearly too few people think about achieving a rapport with their audience. It is a terrible thing to bore the people who have put themselves out to hear you. Thus developing your style to stimulate your audience is, I believe, a duty for public speakers. At least, it is if you ever wish to be invited back.

At first, though, surviving the ordeal is enough.

When you have your basic ideas collected, you must fit them into the time you have available. If you have been asked to speak for ten minutes do so: speaking for twenty may upset the entire schedule of the meeting, or put the audience to sleep, or both. It always annoys me when other speakers drone on without the slightest regard for the attention span of the audience or the effect of their selfishness on others who may be speaking later. Honing your thoughts down is a very good discipline. It helps you structure them in a logical and concise way and limits the possibility of straying from your text. The more well structured your speech, the more comfortable you will feel when delivering it, and the easier it is to return to the argument should your mind go blank for a spell.

If in doubt you can use the old formula: "Tell them what you are going to tell them, tell them, and then tell them what you've told them." In other words a brief introduction to your material, the logical progression of your argument, followed by a brief summation.

If you intend to use facts and figures there are only two rules: use them sparingly and make them relevant and illustrative. Without visual support like charts and slides, statistics can become boring and incomprehensible to an audience. Used well statistics give weight to your argument and make it sound far more scientific, used badly they make you sound like a pedantic bore.

The most difficult thing to do when making a speech is to stop. A final elegant sentence or two can make an otherwise ragged speech seem much more memorable. The worst thing is to grope for a final sentence, not find one and like the pilot who has run out of fuel threaten to crash land, then lurch wildly up again to travel in ever decreasing circles, until both you and the audience feel dizzy. Even if it sounds a little stilted it is better to have a prepared ending point than to seek helplessly for an inspired one on the night and to fail.

The other matter which may make you sick as a parrot is the telling of jokes. Witty and urbane after-dinner speakers make it look easy. It is not. Some people have a natural facility for humour. If you possess this gift treasure it. Most of us, whose palms are sweaty with fear, find it hard to relax into joking. Something that seemed hysterical in rehearsal can become literally so if you blow it on the night. My own rule is to tell jokes only when I feel funny and relaxed and it comes naturally. Otherwise I avoid them like the plague. In my experience most women public speakers tend to be serious, perhaps for the same reason.

Before delivery day, practice. You can do this at home in front of a mirror. You need never admit to a living soul that you have done this. You could also use a tape recorder to get an instant play back, but these often make your voice sound odd and artificial. Whenever I hear my voice on a tape recorder I just hope I do not really sound that awful and do not want to know the truth, but you may sound wonderful.

You will need some kind of aide-mémoire for your speech. Some people write out their speech in full. If this is the only way you can survive, do it. But most people end up reading aloud, rather than speaking to an audience. Reading a speech is a very developed skill—senior politicians and others who have to incorporate a text released to the press into their speeches have to read for accuracy. Skilled speakers can do this without disrupting their flow. Those of us reading from fear are not so relaxed. You may find that your voice disappears into your boots and that you start to mumble. If you have your head down your hair will fall over your face, or your face will be obscured by paper. All this breaks your contact with the audience. If you must write it out in full, then do so, but try to learn the speech by heart and keep the written text as a prompt.

The best method is to use small cards and make your notes on those, in point form. You can refresh your memory without looking down. Your voice will remain audible, and you can maintain the magic commodity of eye contact. Pick out some poor unsuspecting person in the back of the audience and speak to her or him. This will ensure you project your voice to the back of the room. You can shift your gaze from time to time as this makes you look livelier and stops your victim from becoming totally paranoid. It also involves greater sections of the audience. This is a 'trick' but it really does make you look confident and communicative; it makes the audience feel you are speaking to them and have nothing to hide, whereas gazing at the floor makes you look shifty.

The level, pitch and timbre of women's voices can make public speaking more difficult. Fear tends to push the voice into the upper register; if it gets out of control you can start to screech. Deep breathing exercises may help, so does learning to speak from your diaphragm. You may have a friendly voice therapist in your area prepared to give lessons to the group, or drama course tutors, or even enthusiasts from the local amateur dramatics society can provide other sources of help.

Stance and posture affect your image with the audience and your voice. If you face the audience squarely and stand with your legs slightly apart to balance well, your body will be far more relaxed than if you scrunch it up in awkward angles. This also allows your shoulders to relax which in turn opens up your voice by keeping your throat open and the vocal chords relaxed.

If you feel tense and nervous, your shoulders will become raised. This puts pressure on your throat and your voice will sound strained and artificial. If this happens to you practice a few deep sighs. These automatically lower your shoulders and open up your chest and throat. Learning these simple physical techniques will increase your confidence and make you look relaxed and natural.

You may want to use visual aids in your presentation. If you are giving a factual talk illustrations of all kinds help get the information across, help you make your points clearly and help the audience remember it afterwards. You may use maps or charts, a tape slide show or overhead projector, a film or a video. The rule is the same when using technology: you should test all equipment before the start of the meeting and make sure visual aids will be seen by the audience. It is surprising how getting your essential slide on the projector upside down can unnerve you, particularly when you then fail repeated attempts to get it the right way round and people begin to titter. Technology has undone more than one good public speaker and you have to be very confident to take such disasters in your stride.

The only further technicality which may upset you is having to use a microphone. If there are bad acoustics or you are speaking in a large hall a microphone can be very useful. If you get too close up to it you will probably get feed back as well as looking as if you are about to eat it. If you move too far away from it you will be inaudible and if you bob about your voice will alternately boom and disappear which is most disconcerting. Make sure the microphone is at the correct height for you and stand fairly still a few inches away from it. Again, test it before the meeting.

The way you present yourself as a public speaker is just as important as the things you say. Body language will tell your audience a lot about you, as will the clothes you wear. You should be aware of the impression you will make and be sure that you are happy about it. Keep a watch on your mannerisms; it is fine to use your hands when you talk, providing your gesturing is not so wild that it distracts your audience. If you look relaxed it will help relax the audience, whereas a stiff and formal speaker may seem unsympathetic. It will help, once you are at a stage where you can bear it to have a friend watch you for these details and tell you about any annoying habit you may have of which you are sublimely unaware.

The other way to get started in public speaking is to jump into debate when the spirit moves you onto your feet. This is most likely to happen at conferences where there are already a queue of speakers hoping to speak. It is a good way for some people who would be unable to cope with long periods of preparation. In these situations women should push each other to speak through the quick and painless method. It is something I have consistently done throughout my involvement in political and union work, and it is surprising how many women will get up and speak if urged to do so under pressure from sympathetic sources. You have to learn just the right pressure to apply and desist when you feel it is causing distress, but it can work well for some women.

Having got you on your feet through fair means or foul and through the first pain barrier, you must now learn to deal with opposition. It is one thing to speak to an audience direct or as a single speaker, it is another to face opposition. It can come in several forms: if you are unlucky you will suffer hecklers in your audience, or be put down by another speaker, but generally you will find yourself in a formal debate.

Hecklers are difficult to deal with. There are those ready with the witty and winning riposte, I normally think of the perfect thing to say several hours later. In my first meeting as a Union Official with 100 dustmen at 6.45 am one dreary winter day, I was told to "get 'em orf", I ignored it and did not reply as a friend later suggested I should that I had "only just got 'em on". But as a beginner you can handle hecklers by pointing out that you are nervous and rely on your audience's sense of fair play to back you up. I do not necessarily suggest you use this approach when talking to dustmen.

The put-down from another speaker is often devastating. It happens mostly when you ask a question or make a contribution from the floor of a meeting and the speaker replies at the end. You rarely get a chance to come back on him, no matter how much he has humiliated you. This is a carry over from the bullying, sarcastic teacher syndrome in schools. It rarely wins friends in any audience who see it for the unnecessary brutality it is, unless they are politically motivated to crush your point of view through crushing you, in which case hang on in there, your day will come.

Formal debating is impossible to avoid if you want to progress in political life. It is the method used in the corridors of power, hence the 'better' sort of schools and Oxbridge Colleges prepare people, mainly men, to govern the nation through training them in its use. Few women will be practised at debating styles and techniques for they have not been trained up to it. Its rules may seem archaic, but they must be learnt.

A formal debate takes place around a proposition or MOTION. In set piece debates there are at least two main speakers on either side to propose and oppose the motion, but there may be more. There are main proposing and opposing speeches followed by a second proposing and a second opposing speech. When both sides have made their opening speeches, the chair will open up the debate to the floor, taking in logical order, one speech for the motion and one speech against until a thorough debate has been concluded. The chair will then call upon the opposer to sum up, ensuring that the proposer has the last word. Both sides are forbidden from introducing new material into their final speeches. This is supposed to allow for proper and fair debate. The motion is then put to the vote. The procedure is slightly more complicated when the motion has amendments put to it, but this normally happens at conferences and will be dealt with in Chapter 8.

If you are speaking in a context when there is opposition you must deal with the arguments of your opponent. If you are speaking as part of a debating team you must clearly split the arguments up between you and have enough information to destroy the arguments of the other side. You should never be personally abusive; it is against the rules, but would in any case win you no friends.

Public Speaking Exercises

1. Go to a range of meetings to hear speakers. Arrange visits with your group to help with your horizons and experience in general: Local Borough, District or County Council meetings. Trade Union speaker meetings. Political Party public meetings. Try to get to see national figures speaking as well as local activitists. Go back as a parent and visit a speech day to see how well it equates with memory. Listen to after-dinner speakers, visit the local history, literary or cultural societies who hold open talks. Visit the House of Commons, listen to sermons in church.

    At all of these gatherings carry this chart with you and give marks to the speaker.

    (a) Evidence of preparation.
    (b) Balance of factual material to anecdotal.
    (c) Handling of factual material.
    (d) Use of visual aids, how much did they add to performance?
    (e) The speaker's handling of jokes.
    (f) The level of interest in the subject.
    (g) The level of interest aroused by the speaker.
    (h) The speaker's 'body language'.
    (i) The structure of the speech.
    (j) How the speech ended.

    Discuss the results of your individual marking and compare them with those of the others in your group.

2. Take the texts of speeches you have heard made, e.g. if you have visited the House of Commons get hold of a copy of the Hansard of the day you attended and compare your memory of how the speeches sounded with how they look written. You may well find that many speeches look better on paper than they came across on the day, or that a speech that really impressed you is full of waffle.

3. Practise writing speeches in a particular style. Take an agreed subject and each write a speech on it to be given in different contexts, e.g. to the local Conservative Association/Labour Party/SDP Area Party/ Liberal Party Association. The Mothers' Union. The Women's Refuge

Campaign Support Group. The Rotary Club. And so on. Practise giving your speeches to the group.

4. At each meeting assign someone a short talk—perhaps on the subjects in this book—to present at the next meeting. Make sure each one in the group gets a turn. No one is to be allowed to contract out of giving their talk.

5. Set up a formal debate on a 'serious' subject which involves some research. You can either allow people to chose sides by conviction or get them to draw lots for it. When you get more practised invite guest debaters to take part with you.

6. Invite outside guest speakers to your group if there are people you particularly want to hear, or who you think can help you in your pursuit of involvement in public life. It is a good way to get information on opportunities available within organisations.

7. Write up a list of topics individuals in your group have some interest in and knowledge about and send it to local organisations who might be looking for speakers. Start with any organisations of which you are a member and offer yourself as a speaker for them—within your area if it is a national organisation.

8

Making Your Mark
at Conferences

Conferences are strange animals. They are nothing more than a collection
of people clutching papers, put together in close proximity for a period of
time to discuss the problems of the world at large according to the philosophy of the organisation in question. In reality, however, they take on a life
of their own, with their own rules, stars, battles, affections, betrayals and
loyalties. In fact, they resemble a real life soap opera. The activists keep
going on adrenalin and excitement and often little sleep or food and too
much booze. They need to be residential and away from home to have this
affect on people. Then they become a time capsule cut off from the rest of
the world. Indeed, it is possible to forget that a world outside exists and
when they end you blink your way into daylight as the intensity and glory
fade. Afterwards you may wonder what all the fuss was about, but at the
time it is difficult not to become entirely engrossed in it.

There are, of course, all types of conferences. I have concentrated on the
formal policy-making annual conference which many organisations hold.
You probably have to be elected to attend.

Other kinds of conferences abound. Most are less formal occasions,
organised around discussion groups and lectures or talks, but they are
unlikely to have policy-making powers or be representative of an organisation's members. They provide opportunities to explore new ideas and
solutions to problems. This chapter concentrates on formal, policy-making,
conferences because this is where the power lies. Other conferences are open
to more people and help you meet other members of your organisation, to
learn its ropes and to make contacts within it.

The most common response of first-time conference goers is total bewil-
derment. There you are dumped in the milling throng without a clue as to
what is going on or why. Most people are too nervous and vulnerable to
admit to their confusion, everybody else looks like old, experienced hands.
They appear to be following the discussion, know precisely what point on
the agenda has been reached and even laugh in the appropriate places. You,

meanwhile, feel like a martian just landed on a strange planet. The very language, though used with great facility by all and sundry, seems alien and stilted. Lesson one: do not worry, it is reality that has been adjusted to meet some very peculiar conventions. There is nothing wrong with you, but to acclimatise you are going to have to adjust your head to get this strange world in focus.

Adjusting your sights requires an understanding of the mechanics of a conference. Policy conferences have set structures, procedures and methods and these have to be learnt. You may want to change them later, but to intervene to do so you have to use the current rules and regulations. Besides learning the mechanics and how to operate within them, they will teach you from experience how they can be improved to be less forbidding to others.

You will find all the information you need to understand the mechanics of a conference in the constitution, in the section headed 'Annual Conference/ Assembly' or whatever term is used to describe your organisation's decision-making gathering. You will also need a copy of the Standing Orders governing a conference. To understand the content of the conference you will need a copy of the agenda or order paper, the motions and amendments documents, any report of the Executive Committee—including the audited accounts, plus copies of any emergency motions and reports from the conference arrangements committee. Indeed, you may spend the whole conference period balancing impossible documents on your knees, losing your voting card and feeling close to despair. But have faith and all will come clear.

The Constitution outlines the precise powers of the conference and its status. It defines the different sections that make up the conference and outlines their powers and how these are to be implemented. The Standing Orders deal with all remaining procedures to enable the conference to run smoothly and to achieve its purpose. In case no one has made it clear the purpose of a conference is to make policy for the organisation in the alloted time period that will carry it through until the next conference. They are also an annual ritual during which organisations examine their innards, rally the faithful, give space for ego development amongst participants, and in the case of political parties, grab as many of the news headlines as possible.

Your first task is to get hold of all the relevant documents needed. This in itself can often be an ordeal. You should consult the organisation's Secretary to find out how to register for a conference if there is no one in the local branch of the organisation to help you. If possible you should attend conferences as a visitor before attempting to become a delegate/representative at them. Some organisations sponsor their representatives and could be persuaded to sponsor an observer or two. If you cannot get financial sponsorship attending conferences can be an expensive project, particularly where they last for several days and accommodation costs in hotels are added. In these circumstances a day trip might suffice; for your own sanity pick what looks likely to be the most interesting day to attend.

A Conference Dissected

The sections of the Conference are as follows:

1. The Executive Committee

This Committee, whatever it is called, serves the Executive function. It is appointed or elected to implement the decisions of the organisation, to represent the organisation at a national level and to be responsible for the assets of the organisation.

The Executive will be appointed or elected for a specific term of office. Its members may be nationally or regionally appointed or elected, depending upon the structure outlined in the constitution.

The Executive is answerable to the conference where this is the supreme decision-making body and has to report to it on the work carried out in the interim period since the last conference. The conference normally votes to accept or reject this report. The Executive is a very powerful body. You will notice that its members often sit together on a raised platform above the rest of the conference. This elevated status expresses its pre-eminence. It reports on all activities to the conference and whilst people can and do ask questions of the committee it is relatively easy for questions to be deflected, particularly as the Executive member responsible has access to the organisation's officers who are usually expert advisers whilst the poor representative on the floor of the conference has only the notes they can seldom find amongst their bundles of paper.

Executives are supposed to give leadership to an organisation. It is logical that they should do so. They are in a position to have an overview of the organisation, its needs and its direction. They have also concentrated time and effort thinking about these matters consistently over their period of office. If you find that you and they disagree on every issue you should either seek to get a different kind of committee elected or appointed, or admit that you are in the wrong organisation and leave.

However, Executives have been known to be wrong. They are not gods, although their elevated status and position can make them seem infallible. The advice of an old timer in the trade union movement to novices is: "If in doubt, vote against the Executive." This somewhat cynical and negative view is a recognition that it is easier for the Executive to manipulate the conference than it is for anyone else unless they are very determined and organised and can win over half the conference to their point of view. Executive Committees can also get very bloody to ensure they get their own way. It is part of the challenge and the adrenalin run of a conference that this should be so but often seems nonsensical to an uninvolved onlooker. As Executive speakers often conclude debates and advise delegates on how to vote, they can greatly influence the outcome.

The Executive also reports on the financial position of the organisation and presents properly audited accounts.

2. The Chair

The chair is normally the President of the Organisation, who has power to delegate the task of chair to a deputy, so that she or he can take the occasional sanity-restoring break.

Chairing a conference is a similar task to chairing a meeting, but larger. In keeping order in the conference, the chair often has to take a complicated series of points of order from representatives on the floor of the conference. Aggrieved representatives who remain aggrieved have recourse to a number of procedural motions to try to get justice for their case. This rarely happens in any but the most stormy of meetings, but is more likely to happen with huge numbers of people in a conference setting when feelings and temperatures can run high.

Despite being often under attack, the chair has a great deal of power over the structuring of debate and in many cases in deciding who can speak in general debate within the alloted time for policy discussion after motions and amendments have been moved and seconded.

I have been to conferences where, whatever the content of debate, once the chair has reminded the conference how the Executive would like them to vote, the assembled masses behave like Pavlov's dogs. This happens particularly in political parties at or around the time of a General Election when unity is the order of the day and opposition is not to be brooked.

3. Executive Sub-committees

These can either be permanent or temporary. Permanent ones will be mentioned in the constitution and defined. Temporary ones can be set up as working parties or advisory bodies through a motion at a previous conference or even by the Executive Council where the constitution states that this is within its powers.

Permanent committees can include an organisation committee, a Foreign Affairs Committee, separate committees for policy formation, and Finance Committee.

Finance Committees may be sub-committees of the Executive, reporting to it, but they may also be a watch-dog body set up by the conference in which the Executive has some representation. They can be asked to report direct to the conference whether or not the Executive Committee as a whole accepts what they have to say.

Other permanent sub-committees are likely to be of less importance and report through the mechanism of the Executive report with no separate status within the conference itself.

4. The Conference Arrangements Committee

This body has the task of running the conference. It makes sure that all deadlines are met and has the task of informing members of the organisation of the requirements of their participation in the conference. Thus it starts its work long before the conference and finishes it with the final report of the conference sent to members.

This committee comes into its own at the conference where in procedural recommendations it reigns supreme. The Conference Arrangements Committee is supposed to be an independent body elected by the conference and answerable to it alone. It often has representatives from the Executive Committee amongst its members, but is in no sense a sub-committee of the Executive. Its independence is meant to ensure fair play to members of the conference. Where Executives do not have direct representation on the committee they will have an Executive Committee member who liaises with the Conference Arrangements Committee.

This is right and proper, for the Executive must discuss with the committee the time needed for the Executive report back, and the main priorities of policy and so on. Executives normally try to make a puppet of the Conference Arrangements Committee to do its bidding rather than that of conference. Usually, Conference Arrangement Committees, whilst bowing in the direction of the Executive's needs, are extremely good at resisting the political pressure brought to bear on them. When they are not, the ordinary conference member can find that trying to get their point of view across is like doing battle with a juggernaut on a road with no zebra crossing. They get run over and wiped out. This normally only happens to conference members wanting to buck the system in some way, but in extreme cases can happen to any innocent abroad. Where a Conference Arrangements Committee becomes this corrupt it is a good idea to serve it warning and if it does not reform, get rid of it.

Let no one tell you that a Conference Arrangements Committee is not a *political* body. Whilst its job is meant to be procedural it can have vast direct political powers given to it through the provisions in the constitution. Its real potential power is indirect through a subtle manipulation in which the clock is the disciplining force.

The Conference Arrangements Committee have the task of structuring debate, so that order can come from the chaos of several opinions. They form the material submitted by the local branches of the organisation for debate at annual conferences as motions and amendments into a logical progression. They can persuade the representatives of local branches to join forces with others of like position to 'composite', i.e. put together their motions. This saves time and duplication and can act to build the support for a particular position. They may have the power to recommend particular amendments for debate where there is an optimum position which reasonably expresses aspects contained in separate amendments. The Conference Arrangements Committee will have powers to refuse motions if they are not tabled and submitted according to the prescribed rules contained within the standing orders. They can also rule 'out of order' any emergency motion which does not meet the definition required under the standing orders.

The committee reports to conference in the opening session and gets an acceptance to the agenda or order paper for the conference as a whole. This may be further altered during the course of the conference if time runs short or unforeseen events mean a change would be sensible. Once the order paper has been accepted it requires a two-thirds majority of those attending and voting to change it.

Aggrieved members of the conference who disagree with the committee's recommendations, or feel they have been badly treated may have the right to oppose the committee, on the floor of the conference. Challenges to the committee recommendations are decided on one speech for, a reply from the chair of the committee, and a simple majority vote.

Most of the work done by the committee is never seen by ordinary representatives. They work outside the conference and can be in permanent session to determine what recommendations should be made to conference or to oversee the production of conference materials. They may well meet individuals or groups of representatives throughout the conference proceedings to discuss their motions and amendments. They will hold special meetings for aggrieved representatives to see if an acceptable compromise can be worked out. They remain busy throughout the entire conference.

If you get to see the committee it will be because your local branch has submitted a resolution and you are attempting to get it debated on the floor of the conference, against the wishes of the Committee. In this case forewarned about the potential behaviour of such committees is forearmed. Go prepared to do battle.

5. The Body of Conference

The body of conference is made up of the following:

(a) Representatives or Delegates

You will be either a representative or a delegate according to the kind of organisation you are in. Delegates normally have been instructed by their local branch on how to vote on issues and are expected to express the opinion of the branch as a whole rather than their own. In practise this is impossible as many issues will not have been discussed by the local branch: nevertheless they will stand accountable on their return. Representatives also express the views of their local branch where it has put forward a specific motion or amendment, but apart from this they are free to exercise their own judgement. They have probably been elected because their views are representative of the branch as a whole but they are not instructed how to vote.

However they are chosen, and whatever their designation, these people are the official spokespeople for their local branch and act on its behalf at the conference.

They have the right to speak, to propose motions and amendments, and vote at the conference.

As well as representation from local branches, there may be other recognised constituent groups who have the right to elect or appoint representatives. In the Labour Party, for example, there are such groupings which include Trade Union affiliated membership, women's sections and the Co-operative Movements sections. These can represent blocks of power within the organisation.

Some conferences are gatherings of self-selected individuals, as within the Liberal Party. But in these cases the Party Leaders may be under no obligation to take note of their decisions, and even less to act upon them in Parliament or Government.

Some, such as the Conservative Party have conferences which are more like great rallies of support, rather than policy making. Here they debate very short statements rather than detailed policy documents and are not often known to be critical of their leaders.

Hence there are many variations on the theme. More than any other gathering the conference gives you the essence and flavour of the organisations, and the decisions the body of conference make and the way they make them reveal its identity.

(c) Observers and Visitors

These may be the same thing. Sometimes observers are a semi-official category and work with the representatives or delegates. They are sometimes allowed the right to speak, but hardly ever to vote, in elected gatherings.

Visitors are just that and can come from anywhere. Often they do not have to be members of the organisation, but interested outsiders. They usually sit at the back of the conference hall, clearly separate from the main participants. Visitors can include invited guests from home and overseas. Occasionally one of these guests may be invited to address the conference to bring greetings from their organisation. Visitors who are members of the organisation can sometimes speak when general discussion of a non-policy making character takes place.

6. Other Groupings

There may well be other official conference bodies to do with the running of the conference. Some organisations love committees because they give more opportunities to more people to feel raised above the common herd. Some of these may have power, others may be purely functional, and can include:

(a) Appeals Committee

This committee deals with members or local branches who have been disciplined or expelled from the organisation. Any member or local branch so dealt with by the Executive Committee can put in an appeal to the Appeals Committee which considers their case. This committee is normally an elected one. If the member(s) remain aggrieved at their treatment the procedures may allow appeal directly to the conference. The Appeals Committee is formally designated within the constitution.

(b) Credentials Committee

This committee checks people's validity as delegates or representatives and issues voting cards, etc. In most organisations this function is carried out by officials of the organisation acting outside the conference proceedings, or by the Conference Arrangements Committee. Where it exists as a separate committee it can be very officious: like the Spanish Inquisition it hunts down heretics who dare to lose their voting cards.

(c) Other Committees

The more paranoid an organisation the more committees it will have at its conferences. Some even have Security Committees which check delegates in and out of conference sessions. Other variants are Communications Committees and Press Liaison Committees whose function can only be guessed at.

(d) Tellers

Tellers are appointed by the conference and are there to count the votes when a vote is close enough to warrant it. Often the chair cannot decide which way a vote has gone or a conference participant is dissatisfied with the chair's judgement. In this situation a count will be called for. The chair may have absolute right to call for one. There is usually a special procedure for a conference participant to call for one. They may, for example, have to get the support of a specific number of conference participants. All these rules are contained within the Standing Orders. When a vote by show of cards has been called, all voting participants return to their seats whilst the tellers do their stuff. They give the total number of votes both for and against the motion or amendment to the conference chair who then announces it.

(e) The Media

There are often tables at the front of the hall under the Executive Committee platform where members of the Press sit. This is the dreaded media who spend a lot of their lives being reviled from the platform from which conference participants make their speeches in debate.

Time was when only the Labour Party Conference was paranoid about the loathesome media; now almost every political party, voluntary organisation, trade union, employers' group, and even the Church seem to have its problems with the Press. It always seems strange that invitations to accept media hospitality at conferences are accepted with such alacrity. This may be what is meant by cheque book or expense account journalism.

It may be that the front benches are empty for every debate you consider of great social, moral and political importance, but the Press mysteriously turn up whenever there is likely to be a bundle. They have a sixth sense for trouble.

The next day you will read their newspaper reports of the conference and wonder if you have been at the same event. It does not take long to develop a true cynicism about our 'free Press'. Even if much of the criticism is exaggerated it is a favourite conference pastime. The other one is searching for your name in the papers the day after you have made a speech as nonchalantly as possible for the benefit of those sitting around you. Political Parties in particular are getting more serious about media presentation and go in for greater stage management of the annual conference to maximise coverage.

7. Constitutions and Standing Orders

The constitution outlines the law. It is sancrosanct and can only be changed by a specific constitutional proposal which gains the support of a proportion of the conference or membership normally equivalent to two-thirds or more of those eligible to vote. The Constitution may be considered every few years at a specially convened 'Constitutional Conference'.

The Standing Orders are the by-laws. They are set up to ensure the procedures are fair and that the conference can run smoothly, but they are not inviolable and can be suspended when it seems logical to enough people to do so.

When Standing Orders are suspended it is only for a temporary period to allow the discussion of a special proposal or question. Once this question has been decided they are then re-imposed and everything gets back to normal.

If you want to make a point under Standing Orders procedures you rise 'on a point of order'. The Chair has to take all points of order unless a vote is being taken. It would obviously be very confusing to take bits of discussion in the middle of a vote, so the rules state that the only points of order that can be taken during a vote must relate specifically to that vote.

For example, a conference participant may be confused about the effects of passing the amendment at hand on the rest of the debate. Sometimes if an amendment is passed it rules out a later amendment in the debate which directly contradicts it. In such situations the following amendment is said to 'automatically fall'. The chair will clarify the situation before proceeding to the vote.

Points of order can also be used to change the course of debate. The following are motions that can be moved on a point of order. They are known as procedural motions and are aimed at altering the course of debate or at challenging the chair. It usually requires a two-thirds majority to suspend standing orders as the rules have already been accepted along with the order paper at the start of the conference. It requires a simple majority for a procedural motion to be passed, as it is a straightforward resolution like any other and does not change the constitution.

The following are motions on procedure that you may find in the standing orders:

(a) *That the question be now put:* This means that all debate is cut and that the discussion moves straight to a summing up by the mover of the motion and then to a vote. In certain circumstances the summing up might also be cut and the vote taken.

(b) *That the question be not put:* This means the debate simply ends without a vote being taken. This procedure is often used when a decision one way or another would be an embarrassment to the majority of people in the conference.

(c) *That the next question be moved:* This has the effect of moving on to the following debate without taking a vote on the debate in process.

If, as a representative on the floor of the Conference, you feel unjustly treated by the Chair, you can challenge her ruling. This takes a particular kind of nerves of steel and can ruin a truly promising career, or at the very least a potential friendship with the Chair. However, in certain circumstances it may seem necessary. To do it, you should rise on a point of order and declare a challenge to the Chair. The Chair should hand over the chairing of the conference to a colleague. You make your point in a speech; the Chair has the right of reply and the conference decides. This procedure is rarely used. There may be no formal guidance in your constitution for the procedure, but you can be guaranteed a sensational hearing if you attempt it.

Once Standing Orders have been suspended the conference is free to do as it pleases, and, as anarchy could reign, they are only suspended to consider the one specific issue agreed to by the conference. After the conference has debated and decided this issue, Standing Orders are automatically reimposed. It is now unusual for a set number of procedural motions to be defined under an organisation's Standing Orders.

8. The Form of a Conference

Having examined the component parts of the conference, we need to put them together by having a look at the form of the conference. There is a normal pattern to policy-making conferences, and then of course there are variations.

Conferences normally begin with a message of welcome from an official dignatory of the town in which they are being held.

This is certainly the case for all trade unions and party political conferences. But then these have taken the seaside town venue circuit. If the conference is held in a university, for example, depending on its relative importance it might be welcomed by the Vice-Chancellor or a more lowly minion. Then the organisation's dignatories make their opening comments. Often the President will make an opening address, known as a key note speech to set the tone for the coming debate.

After the opening pezaz the Order Paper outlining the conference programme is sorted out. Participants may seek to amend the proposals of the Conference Arrangements Committee. Once this has been adopted by a vote of conference participants, formal business begins, and the conference is formally 'in session'. A session is normally a morning or afternoon, there being two sessions in a single day. At the National Union of Students' conferences there used to be a third session which lasted until midnight, after which the social life started. I do not recommend this for those wishing to survive a five-day conference either physically or mentally intact.

The order paper is worked through consistently. Motions are proposed and sometimes seconded; amendments are moved, and then debate takes place within the time-scale proposed by the Conference Arrangements Committee and agreed by the conference participants. Time-tabling can be all-important, particularly for a conference where the speeches of key people are timed for television and media coverage. At the end of the debate, votes are taken.

Throughout the conference sessions there will be breaks for speeches from dignatories. These are nearly always timed for maximum Press coverage and are part of the business of managing a conference which exists partly for its members, but also to get their message across to the world in the most effective possible way.

At most conferences there are a massive number of fringe meetings. Some are held by outside voluntary campaign groups hoping to have an influence on the thinking of the members of the organisation. Some are held by internal groups seeking an extra platform for their views. You would think that conference participants would have had enough jaw and choose the alternative of lunch and dinner, but something takes over at a conference and it seems that they cannot get to enough meetings. Fringe meetings can be very well attended and do provide a valuable opportunity for interest groups to lobby opinion. Some fringe events are dedicated to the gentle art of alcohol abuse on the expense accounts of big business. There are even organisations who put on breakfast meetings, and drag unsuspecting, probably hungover, invited guests to listen to even more jaw at 8.00 a.m. In my experience of political party conferences, the most interesting political debate goes on at the fringe meetings where people are free to express the views they are cautious enough to keep to themselves or to express vaguely in the accepted code of the day at the conference proper.

After the fringe meeting comes the social life. I have witnessed everything from tea dancing (at lunchtime, no less) through the gamut of reviews and shows, to disco dancing and the off-key maudlin singing in the small hours of those whose stamina is beyond question.

If this is a typical day, put a few days together and you have a picture of the week. You will see why a recovery period is sometimes necessary and pre-conference training a help. They really are very intense periods of time.

Whilst this is a general pattern, there are organisations that vary this diet. The Liberal Party, for example, works through commissions whose task is to prepare a motion for debate at the Assembly which follows their few days' discussion in commission groups. Commissions work from a series of commissioned and volunteered papers. The chair of the commission opens the debate with a report of the commissions work.

9. The Form of Debate

(a) Motions and Amendments

The same principles apply here as apply for meetings in general. The one difference is that you may need to be more precise in your drafting and will have to defend your position in front of larger numbers of people. The deadlines for submitting motions and amendments are final. They cannot be presented at the conference. Only emergency motions can be submitted at the conference and must comply with the rules governing emergency motions, i.e. the event in question must have occurred after the closing date for the submission of motions.

Every organisation has a house style for motions. The best thing to do is to get copies of past agendas which contain motions and amendments which have been debated at the previous conferences of the organisation. Study these and simply follow the formula used by others, even where you dislike the formula. There will be plenty of time to propose change when you have established yourself and feel you know what changes should be made.

(b) Voting

All issues at conferences are resolved by voting. Sometimes votes are taken after every amendment, sometimes they are taken at the end of a debate on a motion and its amendments. Most organisations adopt one of these practices only, rather than mixing when it takes its votes.

Voting is normally done by a show of hands or voting cards.

Some very large organisations have a 'card vote' system on top of a vote by showing delegates' cards. In these organisations the number of members in the local branches are totted up and a collective vote equating to that number given to the branch delegate to cast at the conference when a card vote has been called.

Thus a card vote can mean either the aggregate vote of a local branch or the vote holding up a card by its individual representative or delegate. The aggregate vote is usually called when a vote by individual card has failed to produce the desired victory for the most vocal branches with the largest aggregate numbers. Again, there is a written procedure in the Standing Orders that governs how this should be done.

(c) Speaking at a Conference

The same rules apply that govern speaking in public in general, but here timings are far more severe. Speakers often speak from a podium raised slightly above the body of the hall, but not so high as the elevated position of the Executive Committee. There are often a system of lights on the podium which control the timing. These are green, amber and red for fairly obvious reasons. The green light turns to amber at a point when you should start winding up your speech. The chair will ask you to stop when the red light goes on. Some chairs are softer than others about this, but it is bad practice to go much beyond the red light as the other conference partici-pants have a keen sense of time and will get agitated. It will not help you to win sympathy for your argument to ignore the light system. You should check how long you will have when the amber light goes on as this varies widely between organisations. So, when you are due to make a speech at a conference, time what you have to say as precisely as possible. You will probably only have about 3–6 minutes to make your points.

Logic should tell you that it is not possible to give the encyclopaedic analysis of any problem and its solutions in 3–6 minutes. You can make roughly one point per minute and will need some time to sum up. Only brilliant orators who have their audience eating out of their palms can afford to ignore this advice. Daunting though it may appear—speaking to this discipline will help you to speak concisely in all public speaking engagements and is a very good training for public speakers.

You are only guaranteed the right to speak if you have submitted a motion or amendment which has been picked for debate at the conference. Most conferences have some provision for speakers from the floor. They often operate a series of speakers' slips which you fill out with your name and the subject or motion or amendment on which you would like to speak, and whether you are for or against it. These are handed in to conference stewards or officials. It is often the chair of the debate who decides who will speak. It might be done on a first come first served basis, but often stage management plays a role. In these circumstances it can be an advantage to be a woman. You will notice the small numbers of women who speak in most debates compared to the large number of men. You will also notice that there will be more women on Health and Social Services type debates than men and infinitely more men on the Economy and Defence debates. If the conference is appearing on television the chair is often keenly aware of the image the organisation seeks to portray. One is tempted to say that all members of ethnic minority groups should find a way of indicating this on their speaking application form.

The system of speakers' slips is tricky. You can find that you have spent ages preparing your speech and do not get called. For some people, however, they can put in a slip on the probability that they will not get called and then be forced to speak when they do. Because it has an element of the unpredictable it does not seem so deliberate as a commitment to speak. Lots of women who seemed to be ready to start speaking at conferences, but lacked the final spur, can be persuaded to do so through this method.

10. Getting to be a Conference Representative

You will only get to be a representative or delegate through the rules of your own organisation. This probably means that, unless it is totally moribund, you will have to have been an activist for some time. There are the other categories at conferences, however, and some conferences also have general discussions as well as policy discussions, where visitors can speak. Again, check the rules.

Exercises for Conference Participants

1. Getting the Feel of a Conference

This requires action research. First write down a list of all the sections you would expect to find at conference and watch the television coverage of the TUC and the political party autumn conferences. If you start your training programme at a different time of year, you will have to visit whatever policy-making conferences are available. Trade unions tend to have their conferences in the Spring, followed by the TUC in early September. The CBI Annual Conference takes place in November.

You can apply to go as visitors to these. See if you can locate all the groups you would expect to find. Where does power seem to lie?

It is a very useful exercise to compare the impression given on television coverage with the real thing.

2. Learning the Rules

Take a checklist from each of the sections of this chapter according to your particular interest. For example, from the section on speaking at conferences the checklist might be:

(a) How long is allowed for speeches proposing motions? For Seconding? For proposing amendments? To speakers from the floor?
(b) Is there a time warning system for speakers? How does it work?
(c) How do speakers get to speak?
(d) Are the speakers clear and precise? Do they stick to times? How do the conference react to them?
(e) Does the Executive platform sum up the debate? How does the voting pattern equate with the audiences' expressed response to speakers?
(f) Do the speeches make an appreciable difference to the result?

Take your checklist to the conference and make notes. If you are working with a group compare notes with the rest of the group.

3. Dealing with the Agenda

In your group take the motions for debate at conference. If you are all members of the same organisation, get hold of a copy of motions to your conference. If not write to organisations that interest you for copies of their previous conference agendas. Take some motions on the same subjects. First see if you think they are compatible. Would you composite them?

If so, produce composited motion out of the motions submitted that agree with each other. Then put the motions that disagree into logical order for debate. You will have now ordered debate. Give members of the group the motion or an amendment and ask them to produce the arguments they would use to support the assigned position. Get them to state these arguments to the group following the logical order that the motion and amendments would be taken in according to your ordering of it.

You can also do this exercise with current conference agendas. You can either watch the conference on television or attend the debate as a visitor. Compare the reality of how the debate is structured and the content of the arguments with your prior assessment of them.

4. The Conference Game

You can play this game with up to 50 people. The minimum number for the role play is 10. The first part can be used by any number.

The 'All Purpose Party' is just that. The sections enclosed of the Constitution and Standing Orders are taken from a number of political parties. The elements of the constitution are just about compatible.

The first part of the game is a quiz to test the knowledge of the group on the rules governing the conference. Divide the group into small numbers and get them to read both the Constitution and the Standing Orders and to answer all the questions. Most are factual, some are philosophical. Compare notes at the end by asking each of the small groups in turn to give their answer and then check with the other groups to see if they agree.

Again, if you are all members of the same organisation you can use the relevant section of your own Constitution and Standing Orders. If there are special features of your constitution, adopt the quiz questions to take this into account.

The second part of the game, though designed for quite large numbers can be played by fewer people if one of the debates is dropped. The second part is the conference proper and the idea is to run a conference session through. This is split into two parts. The first part is preparation time, for each of the groups. There are six groups plus a President who chairs the conference, who can also act as facilitator.

The groups are:

(a) The Executive Committee who sit at the top table with the facilitator/Chair, and who will also move the main motion in the defence debate.
(b) The group moving Amendment One.
(c) The group moving Amendment Two.
(d) The group moving the Emergency Motion.
(e) The group moving the Amendment to the Emergency Motion.
(f) The Conference Arrangements Committee.

You will need at least two people in each group, although three or four are preferable. You will also need a facilitator to organise the exercise.

Instructions for Facilitator to Give to Groups

(a) *Instructions for Conference Quiz*

Split into small groups. Read the Constitution and Standing Orders and answer the questions. Then join up groups for a report back. See if you can get the discussion going on the philosophical issues raised by the questions. You have up to 40 minutes for this task.

(b) *Instructions for Conference Game*

The instructions you give will depend on how much time you have. If you want to get them to draft the motions as well you can simply tell them what position they have to put forward in the debate and give them twenty minutes to draft a motion. The major motion on defence should be given to both the other groups who will write amendments to it.

—Group (a) are the Executive who support multilateral disarmament.

—Group (b) are unilateralists.

—Group (c) are both pro-nuclear and pro-NATO and oppose disarmament.

In the emergency debate which is on abortion Group (d) support the 1967 Act, Group (e) oppose it. These motions are already written.

Whilst the two groups write their amendments, the Executive Committee will be discussing how to run the conference. The two Abortion Motion Groups will be meeting members of the Conference Arrangements Committee to decide which motion is the main motion and which the amendment. If you decide to skip this and proceed straight to the next stage, or when all motions and amendments have been written, each group is given twenty to thirty minutes to think through their arguments. Each group makes one proposing speech and one seconding speech in the case of movers of motions, plus one summing up. Movers of Amendments will be able to make one proposing speech and to sum up. In addition members of the groups who are not moving, seconding or summing up will have to speak against other motions and amendments according to the instructions below. When the time allocated is up the conference session is called together. The room should be rearranged into serried ranks of chairs facing the table at which the Executive and the chair sit. The Conference Arrangements Committee sit at a table at the side of the hall.

All the speakers should have been given a time limit for speeches and during the session the speeches should be timed.

If there are any people who have not spoken through the formal arrangements the chair can open up discussion to the floor and invite those who have not done so to contribute.

After the full debate on each subject the Chair conducts the vote.

The All Purpose Political Party

The Constitution: Chapter VIII: Annual Conference

1. Functions

The Annual Conference of the All Purpose Political Party shall be responsible for:

(a) The adoption of policy for the All Purpose Political Party.
(b) Receiving the report from the Executive Committee on its work.
(c) Receiving the financial report from the Party Treasurer.
(d) Receiving the Parliamentary Report from the MP's section.
(e) Exercising such powers as are granted to it by other provisions of this constitution.

2. Composition of Conference

The Conference shall consist of:

(a) The President.
(b) One member elected by each constituent organisation.
(c) One member representing each section/organisation recognised within the constitution.
(d) The Executive Committee.

All elections for representatives shall take place by individual ballot vote.

3. Proceedings of the Conference

(a) The conference shall meet annually on a date to be determined by the Executive.
(b) Emergency meetings of the conference can be called:
  (i) by the President;
  (ii) on the receipt of a written request from 10% of the constituent organisations.
(c) The quorum at any meeting of the conference shall be one-third of its members.
(d) The President or his/her nominee shall take the chair at all conference sessions.
(e) The conference shall debate motions put before it by the policy subcommittee of the Executive Committee. Motions can also be tabled by Constituent Organisations.
(f) Conference shall elect a Conference Arrangements Committee to oversee the smooth running of Conference business.

Standing Orders for the Annual Conference

1. Order for Business

(a) The order of business shall be set out in the conference agenda. It shall be drawn up by the Conference Arrangements Committee which shall propose its acceptance at the start of the conference. The Conference Arrangements Committee shall have the power to propose amendments to the order of business.

(b) Any objection to the proposed order paper shall be debated with one speech for the Conference Arrangements Committee replying to the objection, and settled on a vote requiring a simple majority. After the adoption of the order of business further objections will require a two-thirds majority to overturn the agenda.

2. Structure of Debates

(a) On questions of policy, debate will be based upon a motion from the sub-committee on the policy of the Executive Committee, or from a constituent organisation.

(b) All motions, other than procedural motions, shall be submitted to the conference Secretary, at least two months before the date of the conference. Motions will then be circulated to constituent organisations inviting amendments.

(c) The Conference Arrangements Committee shall select motions for debate from those submitted. The Committee shall have powers to composite motions on the same subject with the agreement of the relevant constituent organisations. If agreement cannot be obtained the Conference Arrangements Committee shall indicate to the conference the motion it proposes for debate.

(d) Emergency motions shall be tabled on the first day of the conference and shall pertain only to matters which have arisen since the closing date for receipt of motions.

(e) Amendments to motions on the agenda must be tabled to the Conference Arrangements Committee two weeks before the conference is to be held.

(f) Conference Arrangements Committees shall select amendments for debate.

(g) Any representative aggrieved at the decisions of the Conference Arrangements Committee not to select a motion, amendment or emergency motion for debate, shall have the right to meet the Conference Arrangements Committee to discuss the matter. Any representative remaining aggrieved has the right to challenge the order paper at the start of each day's business.

(h) The debate on each motion shall be moved by a representative of the President, policy sub-committee of the Executive Committee, or representative chosen by the relevant composite group.

(i) General speakers in debate will be selected by the Chair.

(j) The mover of each motion under debate shall have the right to reply to debate.

3. Speeches

(a) The proposer of a motion shall be allowed to speak for six minutes. The proposer of an amendment shall speak for four minutes. The mover of the motion shall have six minutes for the summing up.

4. Voting

(a) At the beginning of the debate the Chair will indicate if the votes on each amendment are to be taken separately or together at the end of the debate. Votes on amendments will be taken in the order in which the amendments have been debated.

(b) Each member of the conference shall have one vote.

(c) The Chair shall appoint tellers to assist the counting of the vote by a show of voting cards. Votes shall be counted when requested by the chair, or by 25 members of the conference.

(d) If a request for a re-vote is made and supported by 50 members of the conference, it shall be taken.

5. Points of Order

(a) Anyone with speaking rights may raise a point of order. Any point of order must be taken at once, except that during a vote no point of order shall be taken that does not refer to the vote itself. The chair shall put her/his decisions on points of order to the conference.

6. Suspension of Standing Orders

(a) Any standing order may be suspended by a two-thirds majority of conference members voting on a motion. A motion to suspend standing orders must be supported by 50 conference members.

(b) On a point of order conference members can seek to:

  i. Move suspension of standing orders.
  ii. Move next business.
  iii. Move the question be now put.
  iv. Move the question be not put.
  v. Move a challenge to the chair's ruling.

7. Amendment to Standing Orders

(a) These standing orders may be amended by a two-thirds majority of conference members voting on a motion from the President, from the Conference Arrangements Committee, or from Constituent Organisations.

The All Purpose Party Quiz

Answer the following questions:

1. What is the purpose of the Annual Conference?
2. Who can call it?
3. Who decides upon the agenda?
4. Who has the right to submit motions and amendments?
   Will they be automatically debated?
5. How many people have to be present for the conference to be 'in session'?
6. Who is the conference?
7. Who or what is the Conference Arrangement Committee? What does it do?
8. What is a point of order? When can they be raised? What can they do?
9. Who has the most power at the conference?
10. Do you consider the conference to be democratic?
11. Is there anything about the conference procedure you do not like? How would you try to change it?
12. How could you get a motion submitted to conference?

The Conference Groups: Instructions

1. Group i is the Executive Committee and as well as proposing and seconding the main motion, it will also have a speech against Group ii the Unilateralist Group. They will have 45 minutes to write the speeches and decide who is going to speak.

2. Group ii is the Unilateralist Group. They will have one speech proposing the motion, a summing-up speech on their amendment and one speech against the position of the pro-Nato Group (Group iii). They will have 45 minutes to write the speeches and decide who is going to speak.

3. Group iii is the pro-Nato Group. They have one speech proposing their amendment and a summating speech. They also have a speech against the main motion, i.e. that moved by the Executive Committee. They have 45 minutes to write the speeches and to decide who is going to make them.

4. Group iv is the Conference Arrangements Committee. It is their job to decide which of the two emergency motions on abortion should be the main motion and which should be the amendment to it. The only information they have to go on is that at previous conferences decisions have been made to support the 1967 Act. They have 10 minutes to make a decision.

5. Groups v and vi are the pro 1967 Act Group and the anti-Group. Whilst the Conference Arrangements Committee is meeting, these groups meet separately to decide what arguments to put to the Conference Arrangements Committee when they are called. Neither group should be readily prepared to become the amendment to the motion. They have 25 minutes to decide their arguments. The only

information they have is that previous conferences have supported the 1967 Act.

The groups will have 20 minutes with the CAC before the conference starts to reach a conclusion.

All times can be adapted to meet your groups needs. You may want to spend all day on the exercise as a whole.

The All Purpose Political Party

Motion on Defence: Group 1

This conference of the All Purpose Party recognises the need for a positive campaign to ensure—multilateral agreement to arms reduction. The conference calls for an immediate move in NATOs position from 'no early use' of nuclear weapons to a 'no first use' position. In addition the Conference calls for a moratorium on the current deployment of Cruise weapons, and for a freeze on future deployment.

The All Purpose Political Party

Motion on Defence: Group 2

(Delete all and insert)

This conference of the All Purpose Party totally condemns the NATO Alliance for its policy of deployment of Cruise and Pershing missiles and calls for immediate withdrawal of the missiles so far deployed in Western Europe. Further, this conference calls for a rejection of all nuclear weapons on British soil, for withdrawal from NATO and for an end to the Warsaw Pact.

The All Purpose Political Party

Motion on Defence: Group 3

(Delete all and insert)

This conference of the All Purpose Political Party supports the deployment of Cruise missiles throughout Western Europe and calls upon the Party for a vigorous campaign in defence of our NATO Allies. The Party accepts the need for a nuclear defence policy if world conflict is to be avoided, and the necessary deterrence is to be maintained.

The All Purpose Political Party

Emergency Debate on Abortion: Group 1

This conference greets with alarm the news of the latest attempt to restrict the 1967 Abortion Act through the Private Member's Bill sponsored by James Splott, MP. This conference expresses its full support for the 1967 legislation and recognises the need to defend the principle of a woman's right to choose whether or not to have children. This conference will campaign vigorously with all groups wishing to see the retention of the 1967 Act, and for the wide availability of services under the NHS.

The All Purpose Political Party

Emergency Debate on Abortion: Group 2

This conference supports the current attempt of James Splott, MP to sponsor a Private Member's Bill to limit the time availability for abortion granted under the 1967 Abortion Act. The conference recognises that there are many abuses of the 1967 Act, and that the laxity of the time period for legal abortion is a gross abuse. Further, the conference supports the rights of the unborn child and feels that these must be weighed against the rights of the parents.

The All Purpose Party: Annual Conference

Conference Agenda

1. President's Opening Remarks.

2. Conference Arrangements Committee Report:
   Emergency motions debate.

3. Major Conference Debate: Defence Policy

   (a) Main Motion (Executive Committee)
   (b) Amendment One: (Unilateral Group)
   (c) Amendment Two: (NATO Group)

4. Emergency Motions Debate: Abortion

   (a) Main Motion
   (b) Amendment One

5. Announcements.

The All Purpose Party: A Training Day
in Conference Procedure

Organisers' Notes

1. *Initial Session on Party Constitution and Conference Standing Orders*

There should be a short introduction on the purpose of Constitution and Standing Orders, including a close look at the materials supplied. The large group should then divide into small working groups to do the quiz questions already set. Their answers should be written on large sheets of paper that can be put up around the walls. Each small group should elect someone to chair their meeting and a reporter. At the end of the time allocated for the quiz, the large group should meet back together and take a report back. The organisers should attempt to stimulate discussion on Conference procedures where appropriate.

Time for Introduction: 20 minutes.

Time for Small Group Quiz: 30 minutes.

Time for Reporting Back to Large Group: 50–60 minutes.

2. *Simulation Exercise: The Conference*

(a) This exercise is designed to give small groups practise in a number of the vital skills necessary to a conference: dealing with the Conference Arrangements Committee, writing and submitting motions and amendments, using the standing orders, and speaking for motions and opposing motions.

(b) There are three main parts to the Conference: Preparations.

—The Conference Arrangements Committee who meet in session to decide which of two emergency motions on abortion should be taken as the main or substantive motion and which should become the amendment. Having met as a small group the Committee meets with both motion groups to negotiate the order of debate.

—The two groups on the Abortion motion. These groups have 25 minutes to discuss how they can try to ensure that CAC agrees to their motion becoming the main or substantive motion, with the opposing motion as the amendment to it. The individual instructions to the two groups point out that the All Purpose Party has traditionally supported the 1967 Abortion Act. The implication of this is that the main motion should be the one opposing change in legislation. These instructions are written to encourage the disgruntled group to challenge CACs decision on the floor of the conference by suspending standing orders. This is done in a way that leaves each group to sort out what action to take for themselves. After the 25 minutes, during which time they also have to decide who will propose their motion and write a speech, they meet with the CAC to be informed of the decision.

—Finally, there are three groups on the main debate on defence:

(a) The Executive Committee who have the main motion which is a pro-Freeze position.
(b) The second group has a pro-NATO, pro-deployment position.
(c) The third group has a pro-unilateral disarmament position.

Each group will have 45 minutes to decide who is to propose their motion: each group also has a speech opposing one of the other amendments. They should use the time to write the speeches.

All groups are instructed to elect a chair to help them work quickly and efficiently as they have no more than 45 minutes in all to complete their individual instructions.

(c) After all groups have completed the 45-minute exercises, they will then convene into the conference. The chair of the conference should be taken by an experienced person who can operate the standing orders. This person should be joined on the platform by the Executive Committee. (The group that has the main motion on Defence.) This group will speak and operate from the platform. This is designed to point out the relative power between the platform and the floor of the conference. All the other groups are the body of the conference. The formal agenda is included in the papers and all participants should have a copy. They should also have a copy of the voting card.

There is roughly one hour for the conference session, so whilst standing orders indicate that speeches should be 6 or 4 minutes it would probably be better to cut speeches down to 2–3 minutes for a proposing speech, and 1–2 minutes for a speech against. All groups should be made aware at the start that the speeches are not expected to be totally lifelike and packed with statistics. The main point is to give practice of speaking in a simulated environment and to test the ability to put forward an argument clearly.

3. The De-briefing

At the end of the Conference Session as much time as possible should be devoted to summing up the proceedings and pointing out where the participants successfully used standing orders and where they failed to do this. It is not a criticism of people's ability to perform in public, but an analysis of their ability to understand the workings of the conference procedure.

Each group should be asked in turn for their comments on the exercise, and should be encouraged to be self-analytical.

4. Facilitators

If organisers prefer it, they could use a facilitator for each small group whose job is to help them when they get into trouble. It may be preferable to have a number of people who will occasionally check each group to see that they are managing.

5. Additional Materials

The chart to monitor speakers' contributions given in Chapter 5 can also be used with the exercise. This should be given either to one of the team to fill in or to facilitators if these are used.

This should be done twice on two different charts. Once in the small group and once for members of that group in the conference session. These can be compared as part of the de-briefing to see what they indicate about the level of communication at a conference.

9

Getting Your Message Across
to the Public

There may be several reasons why you want to get media coverage. For a lot of people it becomes a necessity only when they are involved in a campaign on behalf of an organisation, or when they become a candidate for election to public office. Whatever the reason, if you wait to find out by trial and error how to do it the campaign will be over long before you get a story accepted.

In most cases you will be trying to get material across locally rather than nationally, but either way the same basic principles apply. You have to know the news networks and how they work before you can break into them. Journalists work to the timetables of the newsroom that employs them. They also work within the philosophy that employs them. This does not mean that they are necessarily, or personally, prejudiced but they do understand when they are unlikely to get a story printed. For example, it would probably be a mistake to try to get a story opposing public female nudity into *The Sun*.

There are a vast range of news outlets in Britain. As well as the national press, radio and television, there are the local equivalents. Regional and local newspapers have been joined by the free news-sheets. Many sections of the local community have their own newspapers: these include the ethnic minority press which whilst they are printed mainly in London have wide distribution throughout the communities scattered around the country.

There is a growing specialist press in just about every arena of health and social welfare as well as the professions and in industry. Organisations also have their own newspapers or journals including trade unions and student unions. Most community and women's organisations have some kind of newsletter. There are literally hundreds of outlets for your message. To get it across you need good organisation and adaptability.

First get to know and understand the networks. Many local newspapers will have a very small news staff working to a tight weekly deadline. They will be hungry for news, but have not got the time or energy to go far afield to get it.

Many community newsletters are run by one person who, however sympathetic, has her or his own problems and priorities. You need to build your own card file index on the local press outlets. You will need to know the title, address and phone number of the publication. Then comes its resources: How many people are engaged in writing stories? How many photographers work for it? You should note the names of any contact you can make on the publication as well as its deadline for going to print. If you hold office in an organisation that could be of interest to the publication, you should attempt to meet with the appropriate journalist or editor. Face to face contact always allows much easier access later on.

Details of press publications can be obtained from directories such as Benns Press Directory or Pimms Media Directory. Your local library will have at least one directory. You will have to fill in the gaps from your own research. You can often find the details of newsletters from national organisations to which the local is affiliated. All publications have to carry the legal imprint stating who publishes it and giving an address, so if all else fails you can write to the named person to supply details.

Having got your basic information system set up, you can concentrate on designing your stories in a way that maximises their chances of being printed. Learn the style of the papers and journals you want to use. Many local papers dwell on social and community issues rather than the hard news that the National Press favours. They also like a good photograph with a story. They have a lot of pages to fill on a regular basis with a small staff, so the more you can give them, and the fewer items they will have to re-work, the better. Stories that can be printed directly are the most likely to get in. You will find the stories in local newspapers are about small day-to-day events that affect the life of the community. There will be reports of local Council Meetings and their decisions, but there are also the 'human interest' stories. Most of the latter have been given to the paper by the people concerned. Journalists do not, by and large, roam the streets looking for the story of the baton-twirling cheerleader at sporting events. I am not suggesting you dress up in this ridiculous fashion to get coverage—particularly if you want to be taken seriously later on—but there are many events that can get this kind of coverage to get you known to the newspaper which may open the space later for more weighty pronouncements. The kind of things that can get coverage are the visit of a national dignitary, a celebration to honour someone with a presentation, charity events and stunts, the election of one of your officials to office in the local community, and elections and appointments within your own organisation. All these events can provide photographs. Children and animals are guaranteed winners—if you can bear it.

Learning to write clear and precise Press Releases is an important part of getting your message across. Journalists like Press Releases because they cut down on work, and the news comes to them. Press Releases alert them to coming events, inform them of important decisions that have been made, provide reports of meetings and conferences, précis reports and circulate speeches. They give reporters a basis from which to work if the material is stimulating enough. So, Press Releases have to be noticed. A news editor on a paper or in a local newsroom may have several hundred Press Releases per day. Many companies and professional organisations employ Press Relations Officers to ensure a constant information flow. You are competing with these people for coverage. Thus your releases should look professional and always be typed.

To put a Press Release together follow the rules that journalists learn. An editor wants to know: who, where, what, when and why, i.e. the name of the person or organisation, what they are going to do, where they will do it, and when, including date and time and finally why it is being done.

Example: Ms Anthea Smith, President of the Somewhere organisation, will be addressing the local meeting of the Somewhere organisation, at the Lower Church Hall on Tuesday, June 3rd at 3.30 p.m. to present the local organisation with a special merit award.

From the local newspapers' point of view the most interesting thing about the story may well be that a local organisation has won a merit award. The story should then be written:

The local Somewhere organisation will receive an award from Mrs Anthea Smith, President of the National Somewhere Organisation at the Lower Church Hall on Tuesday, June 3rd at 3.30 p.m. The award is being made in recognition of the outstanding service of the local Somewhere branch to the national organisation.

As news editors will barely read a press release in full if they have tens or even hundreds on their desks each morning, your first sentence must contain the most important fact.

Press Releases should also have titles which grab the eye. A title for the example above might be:

Local Somewhere Group Wins Coveted Award! or
National President to Visit Local Somewhere Branch

Because news is about people, direct quotes are very popular. They do not have to be deep and meaningful. Their function is to humanise a story. Every Press Release should have one, making sure that the name and function of the person quoted is given. To use our Somewhere example:

The local Somewhere branch Chair, Ms Jones announced: "We are delighted to have won this coveted award. It shows the effort that our members have made over the past year to put Somewhere on the map."

There may be occasions when you want to give information to journalists about a coming event or speech, but do not want them to cover it until the event itself. You both want to secure Press availability for cover at the time, but do not want to spoil the newsworthiness of the event before it takes place. To achieve this you use the 'embargo' system. At the top of the Press Release you state that it is 'Embargoed' until the appropriate time on the appropriate day.

In our example if the event were important enough to get journalists there to cover it, you might not want advance publicity, but a full report after the event. You might then embargo the story until 3.30 p.m. on Tuesday, June 3rd. Embargoes are only used for important items. Government Departments use them for reports sent out in advance to give journalists a chance to study them and respond intelligently, but to stop them doing so before the publication date of the report itself.

If you are going to put an embargo think carefully about it. You do not want to embargo stories in such a way that the release time is after the appropriate deadline date for publication, or for a time when you will make little impact. Knowing this may help you change your priorities when organising events if it is vital to get Press coverage for them.

The Press Release should look professional. It should be on headed notepaper and typed. You should use only one side of A4, clearly dated at the top with a clear embargo date and time before you start the text. You should use double spacing and wide margins to allow the sub-editors to write instructions to printers. Keep sentences from being split between pages and if you use more than one sheet number the subsequent pages and add an identifying mark such as Somewhere 2, Somewhere 3. You may want to get the paper to send a photographer and arrange a picture 'stunt', if so add details to your Release. At the end of the Release write 'ENDS' clearly separate from the text. Always give the name and both day and evening phone numbers of a person who can give further details, normally the person who issued the Release.

Your final Press Release will look like this:

NOWHERE SOMEWHERE BRANCH   12 Church Walk
                                                                      Nowhere

                                                                      May 28th

PRESS RELEASE: EMBARGOED 3.30 p.m. June 3rd

LOCAL SOMEWHERE GROUP WINS COVETED AWARD!

   The Local Somewhere branch is to receive a special award from the organisation's National President, Ms Anthea Smith at a ceremony at the Lower Church Hall on June 3rd. The award is being made in recognition of the outstanding service of the Nowhere Somewhere branch to the National Organisation.
Local Somewhere Branch chair, Ms Jones commented:
   'We are delighted to have won this coveted award. It shows the effort that our members have made over the past year to put Nowhere Somewhere on the map.'

ENDS

Contact: Ms Smith 12345 (Office) 54321 (Home)

   Note for picture editors: Ms Smith will present the award at 4.00 p.m. to a group of members wearing the national Somewhere uniform.

If your local paper cannot get a photographer to you, there is no reason why you cannot get a photograph taken and deliver it to them with details of the meeting.

The second way of getting into print locally is to make use of the letters columns. If you read your local newspaper you will notice that in the run-up to the Council elections a large number of letters appear from people signing themselves as candidates for such and such a ward. Many people read the letters columns of newspapers and it is a useful outlet. If you write in a reasonably provocative manner and start a debate you can often get a sort of 'right to reply'.

If your local papers has an 'Opinions' column write to the editor with some ideas for articles you would like to write and see if you can get commissioned to do a piece. If there is more open access simply write a column and send it in. You could even write to the letters page suggesting an opinion column!

Radio

It is very difficult to get on to radio news bulletins. Whilst most local radio stations have several of these daily they are limited to a few minutes at a time. If you think about the content of the items you will notice that there are very few words used compared with newspapers. It is easier to get interviews done for current affairs and discussion programmes. The principles governing interviews are the same.

Facial and hand gestures do not help on radio for obvious reasons, so you have to say what you mean as precisely as possible. You can always put mistakes right, most interviews are pre-recorded so you can go back and start again. If you get stuck for words and want to re-phrase an answer simply ask the interviewer to stop the tape and start again.

All pre-recorded interviews will be edited. So if the interviewer has to provide a three-minute piece for broadcast, they may take several minutes of discussion. This is why it pays to be precise. The more tightly you answer questions the less likely you are to find crucial bits edited out. If you prevaricate, and try to deal with all the pros and cons of a case the news editor or producer will see it as waffle and your words of wisdom will hit the cutting room floor.

In order to help you phrase your answers to questions you must think about the audience you are addressing. Are you talking to young people, or any particular age group? Are you wanting to shine in the sights of your own membership, or to convince the public in general of your case? Within any listening audience there are several different audiences and you may want to shape your remarks to appeal to specific groupings.

The interviewer will normally be working from a brief, possibly one that you have sent them in the form of a Press Release. Thus they will have an angle on the story. Most interviewers will tell you the questions they intend to ask. You have to get the information you want to give into the answer to these questions in a way that cannot be seen as evasive. You should always ask the interviewer what questions they intend to ask if they do not offer the information. If you do not like any of the questions say so: you may feel it could be better put or that another question is more appropriate. You can negotiate an agreed set of questions.

If the interviewer is one of the breed that likes to put the unfair one in without warning, you will simply have to cope with it. Luckily most interviewers are just doing a job professionally and do not play games.

You can have notes in front of you in a radio studio or when being interviewed, but do not start reading from them, as this 'deadens' your voice. If you speak to the interviewer person to person your voice should be reasonably lively.

The golden rules are: never lose your temper as it tends to make you incoherent, and never be rude to anyone as you automatically lose your case. It is far easier to listen to a pleasant, relaxed voice on radio than a harsh one and listeners are far more likely to agree with a case that is pleasantly and logically put, than one that is aggressively thrust at them.

If the interview is in the studio you have to remember that no one will hear you unless you use the microphone properly. Try to stay at the same distance to it or away from it all the time and do not move around or your voice will be lost. Before you start the interviewer will be asked to take your voice level. If you use that test as a satisfactory pitch and level for your voice it will give you the best guideline. Do not make unnecessary noise, blowing your nose into the ears of the nation is not good PR.

If you are asked to take part in a studio discussion or phone-in, accept. It is in these situations that our assertiveness training should be brought into play. You will have to be prepared to intervene in the discussion. If there is a chair to the discussion indicate your wish to speak. The best discussion chairs are very good at bringing people in and if you abide by their rules you will be asked back. Where the chair is bad, you have to get into the discussion by yourself. There are many practised microphone hoggers around, so often, waiting for a natural gap in their sentences is a waste of time. Interrupt as politely as possible. Most discussion programmes last around 30 minutes, this time goes very quickly so you have to make your impact without waiting too long. Constant interrupters, however, simply annoy the listening audience because it jars on the ears when two or three people are trying to speak at the same time. Before the programme ask the Chair how they would prefer you to indicate your wish to speak. If they ignore your agreed signal for too long, jump in.

Phone-ins can be tricky because you do not know the viewpoint of the questioner, unless they make this very clear. Always err on the side of caution when making assumptions about their views. They might just be asking questions in stilted language because they are on radio. I once had a question from someone who sounded like a terrible racist and who was deeply affronted when I treated him as such. He had used a stereotyped way of referring to ethnic minorities as 'our coloured brothers'. I assumed he was being sarcastic. It turned out he was using an archaic and mistaken but genuinely meant trade union type of address. I answered him sharply and came across as narrow-minded and unsympathetic. To avoid repeating my mistake find some praise for the question put to you and then gently disagree with the views expressed by the questioner. Always note the name of the caller and speak directly to them in your reply.

In these programmes you have a set of head phones so that you can hear the caller and a pad and pencil to note down points they make. Nevertheless your response must be immediate. This means you should have prepared thoroughly before you go on. Know the subject you will be dealing with from all angles and get friends to throw hostile and testing questions at you which you must answer immediately. You can also try to ensure some friendly questions by getting friends and colleagues to phone in.

Television

Many of the same rules apply to television as for radio, but because the networks cover far wider regions and have less local input, it can be far more pressurised. Very few people appear on television regularly, so the chances of becoming experienced are limited.

You will meet a vast and confusing array of people connected with any television interview. Your biggest contact will be with the researchers who do the basic journalist's job of putting the facts of a story together. They are under control of a producer (many of these titles change from Company to Company and between the Independent Companies and the BBC). A producer is responsible to an editor. There will probably be a presenter who does the interview. There are then the technicians, camera crews, sound and studio floor managers. The rules of the interview are the same as for radio with the extension of the need to be aware of the visual effect you make. Thus when you think through the major points you want to make and to whom you are speaking, you must also think of the setting in which you are being filmed or interviewed live.

Television makes its impact through images, so think about the image you want to portray. For example, if you are being interviewed about pornography the producer may suggest you be filmed outside a sex shop. You would be unwise to accept. Always try to be filmed with book lined shelves behind you as this always makes you look weighty and authoritative. You can try to negotiate the setting for the film, but it is difficult as film crews have tight schedules and are immensely expensive, so unless your appearance is crucial companies will not pay vast sums to fulfil your wishes. You must always find out what restraints are imposed on the producer by the practical problems of making a film and then negotiate within those parameters.

You must get the intention of the producer clear before being interviewed. You can ask how they are intending to introduce you if it is a live interview, and protest if you disagree with the description. You can ask who else is being interviewed in the programme and the point of view they have taken. Mostly you will be told these facts and they will help prepare the slant of your contribution.

If you have never been in a television studio before ask the researcher to show you around and describe the technical process to you before the interview takes place. You will undoubtedly be offered a drink if the interview is in the evening, and often when it is not. Follow your own dictates but do remember that even a little alcohol can go to your head in an unfamiliar and tense situation.

When you appear on television you have to think about your appearance because it dictates how you will come across. If you feel comfortable and reasonably smart you will also be more comfortable. Unless you wear some make-up you will look pale and ghostly, so you can expect to be sent to the make-up department but you can ask for as little make up as it is possible to get away with.

If you feel strongly about it insist on it, but do not take it out on the make-up artist—the dictates of television are not her fault, and besides it can be quite pleasant to be so indulged. Presenting an attractive personality helps you win the argument. This goes as much for your style of delivery as it does for your style of dress.

During the interview listen to the interviewer's questions and always look at her/him. If you are appearing with another guest, look at her/him and listen when she/he speaks. Never gaze blankly round the studio because there will probably be three cameras and from time to time one of them will pan in on you to get your reaction. If you are unaware of this the viewers may see you as both gormless and rude.

Make sure you keep your contributions and answers brief and to the point. Treat it as a friendly conversation. You are free to disagree with the interviewer and to point out when you think they have made an inaccurate statement, but you must at all times be polite, if firm.

One of the most difficult things for women is to interrupt in a panel discussion. Their answers are often very good but at the end of a programme they have not made as strong an impact as some of the men whose answers can be waffly, but who have put across the image of presence and authority. You have to find a gambit that gets you into the conversation. "I find what Mr Smith said interesting, but cannot agree with it because . . ." or "I do agree with Mr Jones. The most important fact of the case is . . ." In other words, take their ground and divert it.

It is unwise to take notes into a television studio, you will look like an amateur who does not know their stuff, if the notes can be seen.

Again keep an eye on the time. You can make a massive impact if you try to get the last word. If you watch the floor manager you will see them make signals for winding up the programme from 60 seconds to go, onwards. If you can make a strong final point, yours will be the image that remains with the viewer.

If the interview is being filmed or pre-recorded, you will be asked to do some shots of nodding at the interviewer or the other participant(s) if being interviewed with other people. These are for use in the editing process.

General Rules for Dealing with the Media

1. If you want to get into print or to be interviewed on radio or television always be available. You can negotiate how to fit in to schedules, but fit in you must. There is always someone else to interview.
2. If you receive a phone message from a journalist, radio or TV company, always phone back. It is common courtesy anyway, but if you do not contact them they will not bother you again.
3. If you are asked to comment for a news story, always respond. You do not have to give an immediate answer. You can always ask to phone back in a few minutes when you have collected your thoughts, but make sure you do because they may otherwise report that you were unavailable to comment and it will look as if you have something to hide.
4. Remember that journalists have tight timetables and heavy schedules. The easier you make things for them, the more they are likely to use your material and stories in future.

Leaflets

Getting your message across may be a much simpler business of producing a leaflet for general public consumption, or for a specific section of the local community.

All too often leaflets are produced on the assumption that the public has the same assumptions and obsessions as the group producing the leaflet. This guarantees a filing under 'D' for dustbin in most households. As a lot of hard work goes into leaflet production, this seems a pity.

Your material must be geared towards your audience and your distribution as reasonably accurate as it can be to get to those people. If you are wanting to say something to young people you may know that the best place to get to them is the local disco on a Friday night, but they may not be in the most receptive mood for your message in that context. Outside schools and colleges might be better, or town centre shopping on a Saturday.

There will be youth centres and clubs and they may be prepared to take a supply of leaflets from you to put on tables.

Leaflets can only contain brief messages. There is nothing more off-putting than a sheet of A4 filled with single space typing. Where possible you should break up the text with headlines and illustrations, cartoons and photographs. Always remember to put the imprint (i.e. the name and address of the publisher, the organisation and the printer) on the bottom of the leaflet and if you want people to join your organisation or follow up the issues raised, give a contact name and phone number of someone who is available to answer.

You must also think about your distribution system for getting a leaflet out. It really is hard work to slog around lots of streets on your own delivering through postboxes. A team of people who have a regular commitment to getting leaflets out makes the job much easier. It might be more important to build this initially than to rush into mad leaflet production, ending up with piles of paper that no one will ever see. If you are a lonely voice wanting to build allies make sure your initial leaflets are geared to doing just that. Put in a request for help and give a contact point.

Exercises in Dealing with the Media

Deciding on your priorities for a training programme on the use of the media is a totally practical affair. There really is no point spending a great deal of money on training for television presentation if you are highly unlikely to be asked to appear on television. Most people will deal mainly with the local press and should learn how to communicate with local radio stations as these are valuable resources and often underused.

1. In your group decide upon an issue you want to highlight: it could be the closure of a local hospital, or a story that illustrates the needs of the elderly in the community—you could even pick a story from the local newspapers. Get members of your group to discuss what approach they should have to produce a leaflet aimed at (a) women at home with young children; (b) commuters; (c) professional workers dealing with the chosen subject area.
2. Take the stories you have chosen and practise writing press releases in the styles of the various local newspapers. Think out ideas as to what pictures could best illustrate the story and plan how you could set these up.
3. Set yourself the task of getting coverage for the activities of your group within the local newspapers. See if you can establish contacts

with a sympathetic journalist to cover your activities. This exercise goes on until you have succeeded.

4. You can practise your own interviews with the aid of a good tape machine. It is best to work in pairs so that each person gets experience of interviewing and being interviewed. You should, in any case, start on this simple exercise. If you can get a sympathetic radio journalist to come to interview members of the group on a range of subjects this will help. Best of all is to get access to a radio studio. It might just be worth writing to the local radio station to see if they are prepared to take you round a studio and take part in mock interviews. As many local radio stations want to be seen to play a socially useful function there could be good publicity in it for them should they agree to help you.

Some local radio stations also have an access policy of enabling listeners to make their own programmes for broadcast. Perhaps your group could make a programme on women in public life in the local community to explain your aims through the access programme. If you are all members of the same organisation you could attempt to get airtime for your organisation's work.

5. You can use video cameras and equipment to set up quite reasonable simulations of interviews, but you will probably need to get someone with experience to conduct the interviews for you. The bonus of using video equipment is that you can play back the interview and join in the criticism of your performance. You can also practice the techniques of panel discussions and interviews. You may know someone with video equipment and cameras, or may be able to hire it locally. Many local colleges have media courses and access to such equipment. There may be a friendly local woman broadaster who is prepared to help you, or organisations like Women in Media may be able to supply an interviewer. There are a number of private studios that can be rented, but this is often a very expensive project.

10

Becoming a Candidate

Very few women put themselves forward as candidates for selection at either local council or Parliamentary elections. The reasons for this are varied. In general candidates for political office are expected to be amongst the more active members of their political parties; they are also likely to be reasonably well known. Women's home responsibilities, particularly if combined with jobs, leave little time for the level of political activity required to become an established party activist. Even where women are keen to stand for office they may be unfamiliar with the procedures required and find it difficult to get help, advice, and more importantly the encouragement to proceed.

Most Political Parties keep a list of approved Parliamentary Candidates. This is the first hurdle to overcome. Applications to the list are interviewed by senior figures within the Party's structures. If their applications are accepted after interview their names join the central candidates list. Once your name is on the list you are notified of all vacancies for Parliamentary Candidates and may then apply for consideration by the local party organisation. The system of keeping a central list is meant to ensure that only people acceptable to the party as a whole are likely to end up representing it in the House of Commons.

There are, however, variations on this general rule:

The Conservative Party

Applicants have to be proposed by two MPs or two Peers. A new system of regional boards has been recently introduced. These will be held once a quarter.

The Labour Party

There are two lists of applicants the 'B' list of applicants who propose themselves and the 'A' list of candidates who have obtained sponsorship from trade unions.

The Liberal Party

Applicants are self-nominating and are interviewed by Regional Interview Boards.

The Social Democratic Party

Applicants are self-nominating and are interviewed by a panel for inclusion on the Candidates' Panel.

The Scottish National Party

Members become eligible for approval by the National Executive Committee to be adopted as a Parliamentary Candidate after ten months' membership. Branches and Constituency organisations can nominate members for consideration only in the constituency they cover.

Plaid Cymru

Nominations are set in motion by the Pwyllgor Rhanbarth or Pwyllgor Ethiolaeth. Vacancies are advertised in Plaid Cymru publications. Any branch in the constituency may nominate one or more candidates providing that they are nominated by a properly constituted branch meeting.

Green Party

The local party organisation decides which election it will fight and whom the candidate will be. Individuals wishing to stand for election in an area with no local party organisation must do so in agreement with the Area Co-ordinator or the Party Agent.

Getting on to the Candidates' Panel or List is stage one of the procedure. Stage two: getting adopted to fight a constituency is more difficult. Selection procedures for a seat for each political party are different, but in nearly all cases the local party organisation draws up a short list of candidates applying who are then interviewed either by a panel or given the opportunity to speak to a general meeting and answer questions.

This two-step process of becoming a candidate requires a different approach at each level. In the initial stage the task is to convince the political party that you would make a convincing candidate on its behalf. The second stage requires convincing the local constituency or party grouping that you would make a good candidate in that seat. It means that you have to get to know the problems of the constituency in which you wish to be a candidate. You need to find a contact within the constituency who can brief you on local problems and personalities within the local party. You should seek to do some research in addition, and visit the constituency before your interview. To maximise your chances of being shortlisted, you might want to specifically angle your application to the local party to take account of constituency problems.

The problem for women in completing application forms is that often their CVs are quite restrictive compared to those of the men with whom they are in competition. Experience of periods away from work looking after children cut little ice when male applicants have an enormous list of committee responsibilities, public appearances and media exposure. Thus women are often not included on short lists and fail to make it through the first hurdle. Ironically most political parties are now acutely aware of their lack of women on candidates lists and women may have a positive advantage in getting to stage one to make up the paltry numbers in comparison with those of men.

Even so the numbers of women in comparison to men is not impressive. The Parties' approved candidates lists for 1985 are not much improved from the lists at the time of the 1983 General Election. Out of 250 approved candidates for the Conservative Party, 50 are women. The Liberal Party has 63 women out of 533 approved candidates and the SDP 89 women out of 400. At the time of writing the Labour Party's lists were not updated.

In the 1983 General Election there was a total of 2,573 candidates standing for election. The table below outlines just how few women stood:

Table showing Numbers of Male and Female Candidates by Party in 1983 General Election

	Number of Candidates	Men	Women	Women as % of whole
Conservative	633*	593	40	6.3
Labour	633	555	78	12.3
Liberal	322	290	32	9.9
SDP	311	267	44	14.1
Green Party	109	84	25	23.1
Plaid Cymru	38	31	7	18.4
Scottish National Party	72	63	9	12.5
National Front	60	54	6	18.1
Communist	35	30	5	14.2
Other	360	330	30	8.1
All	2573	2297	276	10.7

* minus the Ulster seats

Political parties are becoming conscious of the need to promote women and are discussing positive action as a means to do so. My own party the SDP has a constitutional requirement ensuring that there is a minimum of two women on every Parliamentary shortlist. It helps women gain experience and ensures them a hearing even where their CVs do not make them look as impressive as men on paper. Shortlisting committees get used to having to place women on their lists and selection panels and meetings get used to viewing women as serious potential candidates. They accept what we have known statistically for some time, that there is no evidence of a vote against women as candidates on the part of voters.

Other parties are introducing such measures to help women. But positive action alone is not enough to overcome the other problems women face as well as direct discrimination.

Hence there are a growing number of self-help networks between women in political parties. They can make information on vacant seats available to women, as well as provide contacts in the constituency, and train members to face selection panels and meetings.

Becoming a candidate for local government is both easier and more immediately accessible for women. Whilst such seats are often hotly contested there are many stories of the 'paper' candidates who won by mistake and then embarked on successful political careers.

Selection for these seats is more likely to take place at a very local level in the ward group or constituency party where you live. Local government electoral units are split into ward areas which can have between 1 and 4 councillors to elect depending upon their size and population. In some Councils election takes place every four years; in others a third of all council seats are up for election annually.

Local government includes all the levels from Parish Council, to District and County Councils. All local government deals with services to the community ranging from technical services such as highways repairs, parks and gardens, and refuse collection, through to the caring services such as meals on wheels and home helps. Local authorities outside the Inner London Education Authority also have responsibility for providing education. Local government also deals with planning permission for building. The Municipal Yearbook, published every year and available in most public libraries, is an invaluable publication which outlines the responsibilities of each level of local government and gives a profile of each local authority, its committee structure and current membership.

Most Council business is handled by a number of committees each of which has its own chair and representatives of all the political parties elected to the Council. The committees have a great deal of power to run their own affairs, and often set up a series of sub-committees on specific topics. The committees report to the full Council.

As well as having membership on one or more Council committees, councillors can expect to serve on other bodies within the local community such as on the Boards of Governors of schools and colleges, on community health councils and District Health Authorities, and on such bodies as Community Relations Councils. They will then have a number of problems brought to them by the electors they represent; often councillors hold a local surgery where voters can meet them and discuss problems, and from which much of their casework emerges.

If you intend to stand as a candidate in local government elections you can become familiar with the work of the council and the committees which are of particular interest to you. All papers for council meetings are placed in local libraries. You can be put on to a mailing list to receive such papers by contacting the Town Clerk, although your party is probably already in receipt of these. Most committee meetings and council meetings are open to the public, so that you can observe business being carried out.

The one golden rule to remember when standing as candidate is to be positive about your experience and views. There is no reason why experience in home management and with children when combined with a keen interest in politics should not be adequate qualification for the job. At the same time you have to be aware of the nature of the competition, and that unless your party holds interviews at this stage those who will be shortlisting only have written information to go on. They do not know that you have a personality that will knock the opposition sideways unless you find a way of letting them know that.

Thus you will need to maximise the skills that your experience has given you. You will also need to stress those areas of experience you have that will be considered more valid by what is likely to be a heavily male-dominated selection panel. Such a panel will probably have cut its teeth on the adage that if you select a man as candidate you get the wife and children thrown in, whereas there are no such guarantees the other way round.

There is no doubt that women in their various political parties should be examining the barriers to women taking on roles and positions of power and doing something about it: but rather than just hoping for policy changes, or structural changes, they can offer each other far more practical help than they currently do. All parties have some kind of Candidate Association which exists for a variety of purposes. One of these is to help candidates become adequately trained to their task. It could well be time for more organised women's groups and networks within these bodies to appeal to more women to join their ranks.

When it comes to the choice to become a candidate, there is often a parting of the ways amongst women who have been able to train together to develop public life skills. It is the point at which political differences take over and people look to their own political party to supply them with the skills they need to go further. If your group has a member who wishes to be a candidate the group as a whole may be prepared to help her achieve her ambition, but it is highly unlikely that the political party would allow intervention beyond this point or that there would not be considerable tensions with the group unless all its members shared similar political persuasion. This is not necessarily the case in other countries. In the USA, for example, the National Organisation of Women raises money and support for women candidates regardless of their party affiliation, but it does not yet seem that we in Britain could do likewise in our current political climate.

If your group does want to help, its training tasks are a matter of political and practical organisation to promote the group member using the skills you have developed. These will include:

—Finding out from other candidates what questions are asked by interview panels, and what form the interview takes.
—Writing an application form that maximises experience and political skills.

—Grooming the candidate for interview to get her used to a simulated panel situation.

—Getting information on constituency vacancies and finding contacts in the particular constituency.

—Helping to research the problems of the particular constituency, in order to build a profile for the candidate.

—Finding out information on other candidates on the short list so that your candidate has an idea of their strengths and weaknesses.

11

Conclusion:
Strategies for Power

Whilst I believe training to be necessary and valuable, I also know that preparing ourselves for power is only one part of the solution. There is still a great deal of direct and indirect discrimination against women in the world. This can only be overcome by organising for change. To take on the many roles that women have to play and have power, requires support systems and networks, as well as resources for childcare and the many other forms of care that women supply within the community and the family.

In the climate of the 1980s, campaigning for change has an urgency which was lacking in the 60s and 70s when it was assumed that change was inevitable, but when there was greater evidence of activity. The style of campaigning needs to be different: we can no longer indulge in the more esoteric ideological debate without losing the opportunities to make real, practical gains and the potential allies needed to win them.

Put simply: women need women and, despite the splits and divisions in the contemporary women's movement, there are major opportunities to unite them all. Campaigning for women in public life is just one such platform. Feminism has, after all, had a massive impact on the lives and ideas of women way outside the range of their immediate life style.

Even a cursory examination of the policies developed by women and their organisations from Church Groups to Trade Unions shows a formidable area of agreement on what should be done. Somehow it never gets done. Women seem as little able to work together to get things done as they seem to be in agreement what they should get done. Women's organisations are split between those who want to keep out of politics and those that are up to their necks in committed politics. Those that want out of politics do so because they fear their members will be divided by any sign of political attachment or activity. Those that are very involved are most often ideologically attached to a particular political point of view. In the UK politics is dominated by class considerations: whatever the agreements between women as women they are divided by class loyalties and party ties. Until they learn to work more closely together their concerns as women within their own political parties will continue to be swept aside by the concerns of men. When it comes to women most of our Politicians, our activists and our Political Parties are conservative and scared of change. Thus apolitical women's organisations are scared by politics, and political women are by and large contained.

There are few arenas where women's organisation come together to organise together. There are some passive ones where they come together to share views. The more activist style of the Women's Liberation Movement organisation developed since the late 1960s has led campaigns on women's issues, but they are often dominated by separatists who do not accept that the majority of women will want to continue living with men despite their warts. This has made some sections of the feminist movement incapable of creating an active sympathy with women at the cenre and on the right of democratic politics. Often separatists have the kind of contempt for women's lives that breeds an answering alienation. We have all seen dastardly deeds done in the name of sisterhood, that ultimately undermine and undervalue women.

The consciously feminist movement produced in the late 60s operates on the fringe of politics. At best it has an association with the socialist left. There has been a real vacuum for political campaigning at the centre of politics and the possibility of uniting across the spectrum has been non-existent. There are now organisations such as the 300 Group which have enough clout to involve women and to focus public political attention upon its goals. Developments like this show how far women's ideas have shifted in the last twenty years: the debate now is how to organise around them.

Women's politics in the UK have been characterised by the same sectarianism that conditions the politics of men. Women currently occasionally nod to each other over their party divides, and grimace to each other behind the backs of their male colleagues, but they do not join forces.

We need an agency or agencies that will promote women across the spectrum in professional, public and political life. We must develop a 'girls of all ages' network or networks to help and promote women, who are prepared to put pressure on everywhere to ensure a fair distribution of opportunities. Official bodies such as the Equal Opportunities Commission provide sterling research and education work, but have neither the teeth nor the legislative framework to do more. Agencies and networks must be independent if they are to coordinate the efforts of the women in the fields relevant to them.

The politics of self-help which arose from feminism are now being adopted. Professional women's networks are becoming more sophisticated, and increasingly sympathetic to a more clearly articulated women's politics. Despite these changes it may still not yet be possible to overcome the sectarian political climate. If this blocks the development of a single agency for change, then we must at least work for agreed strategies that different agencies can coordinate.

A strategy for redistributing power could include:

Positive Action Policies

Equal Opportunities in Employment

If we want to see women making it to the top we have to clear the channels through which they can make their journey. Ultimately the career path for women will be as crucial as it has been for men.

The techniques already developed by some employers and advisers of monitoring all data and testing their strategies for creating equal opportunity regularly in practice need to be implemented more widely. Employers should adopt a set of 'equality targets' and measure their progress towards them. Job structures and working conditions should be changed to reflect women's needs, including those for flexibility and part-time work and work sharing at high status levels to fit in family commitments. Executive packages that include child care provision and increased maternity and childcare leave for either parent can help to change the pattern of employment. We must also build the steps of the ladder in a way that helps those who could not yet stand on its bottom rung.

Equal Opportunity in Organisations

Women should be working for increased participation, from women in the professional and trade union organisations. They should seek greater representation on power bodies through measures such as reserved seats for women at every level of the organisation.

Positive Action in Education and Training

We should seek increased resources for special education and training provision in jobs and professions where women are under-represented. We need to recognise that training enhances women's skills and builds their confidence to continue to work for success. Wherever possible we should be developing self-help networks to help women develop political and public life skills.

A Women's Network

At the very least we need to have lists of women's expertise and to promote those women with appropriate skills to public appointment, through the political parties and other organisations to which they belong. Women's groups inside organisations can undertake this role and lobby their own organisation to endorse the names for such promotion.

Helping Women to Qualify

As well as giving women the necessary skills we must help them to promote themselves. The way women present their experience must make it look as good and as relevant as that of the men with whom they are in competition. Inside organisations we can act as an advice and guidance service for one another to pool our experience of selection procedures. We can put women in touch with others who could help them.

Bombarding the Minister

Women across organisations could agree on their own goals for increasing women's participation. The DHSS for example, which has a better record than some in promoting women, could be bombarded with lists of women qualified to act on its advisory bodies. Parliamentary contacts can be used to ask questions of the Minister to monitor progress and to bring the level of applications in comparison to the success rate to public attention. Similar tactics can be used at local level or within organisations.

Encouraging Women to Stand

Our system for government does make it harder for women to help each other than systems elsewhere. A PR system is a positive boon to women. Despite its absence, women must be prepared to encourage those they disagree with on other counts to stand for office within their own parties and to stand as candidates for election. We may end up fighting each other at the polls, but at least we can give each other that first boost into public life.

Giving Women Independent Means

Until women have an income in their own right and are taxed separately as citizens in their own right, we will not make much progress with their status, their resources or their self-image.

My personal belief is that this time round, women are serious about changing the world and are determined to succeed in all walks of life. I do not underestimate the odds against us, but the new ingredient is our will to overcome them. We are no longer our own 'worst enemies', no longer 'queen bees', or underminers of other women—but until we combine our forces to take on the bastions of power in what are still largely male institutions, we will not become our own best friends.

My conclusion is that men must change; must share wealth and power with us, but that nowhere are they queuing up to hand over to us our own fair share in recognition of the historical injustice of their hold on power and our exclusion from it. We have to learn, as every movement for change has had to learn, that if you want power you have to take it. We will have to compete on the same terms as men; train ourselves up to it, and support each other through it. As more and more women are in a position to take decisions the going should become a little easier for the next generation as the pioneers implement policies that support and assist women. I also believe that a fairer share of power for women equals a fairer balance of living for men: it might, however, take them slightly longer to realise it.

Further Reading

1. Women in Public Life

Simple Steps to Public Life. Pamela Anderson, Mary Stott and Fay Weldon. Virago (1980).

Women's Committees: A Study of Gender and Local Government Policy Formation. Shiela Button. Obtainable from School for Advanced Urban Studies, Bristol.

Women Into Citizen. Melville Currell. N. J. Rowman and Littlefield Inc. (1974).

The Divided House: Women at Westminster. Melanie Phillips. Sidgwick and Jackson (1980).

Women, Power and Politics. Margaret Stacey and Marion Price. Tavistock (1981).

Women In The House. Elizabeth Vallance. Athlone Press (1979).

2. Politics and Government

Local Government in Britain: Everyone's Guide to how it all Works. Tony Byrne. Penguin (1985).

Sweet Freedom. A. Coote and B. Campbell. Picador (1982).

Governing Britain. A. H. Hanson and M. Walles. Fontana (1984).

The British M.P. Colin Mellors. Saxon House (1978).

The Municipal Year Book and Public Services Directory. Municipal Publications. Annually.

The Election Book. C. Pick. MacDonald and Co. Ltd. (1981).

Man Made Language. Dale Spender. Pandora (1980).

3. Public Life Skills

Person to Person—Ways of Communicating. M. Argyle and P. Trower. Harper and Row (1979).

You're on Next. M. Bland. Kogan Press (1983).

Public Speaking. D. Castle and J. Ward. Hodder and Stoughton (1983).

A.B.C. of Chairmanship. W. N. Citrine. N.C.L.C. Publishing Society Ltd. (1952).

A Woman In Her Own Right: Assertiveness and You. Anne Dickson. Quartet (1982).

Meetings, Meetings. Winston Fletcher. Hodder and Stoughton (1984).
How To Take Minutes. H. Graham-Helwigh. Pitman Publishing (1957).
Using the Media. Denis McShane. Pluto Press (1979).
The Skills of Negotiating. B. Scott. Gower (1983).
The Right Way To Conduct Meetings, Conferences and Discussion. H. M. Taylor and A. G. Mears. Paperfront (1984).

Index